PROTECTING AGAI[...]

OF NUCLEAR, BIOLOGICAL, AND CHEMICAL WEAPONS

PROTECTING AGAINST THE SPREAD OF NUCLEAR, BIOLOGICAL, AND CHEMICAL WEAPONS

AN ACTION AGENDA FOR THE GLOBAL PARTNERSHIP

Volume 4: Russian Perspectives and Priorities

Project Directors
Robert J. Einhorn
Michèle A. Flournoy

Principal Project Sponsor
Nuclear Threat Initiative,
Washington, D.C.

Published in cooperation with the
PIR Center for Policy Studies in Russia

January 2003

About CSIS

For four decades, the Center for Strategic and International Studies (CSIS) has been dedicated to providing world leaders with strategic insights on—and policy solutions to—current and emerging global issues.

CSIS is led by John J. Hamre, former U.S. deputy secretary of defense. It is guided by a board of trustees chaired by former U.S. senator Sam Nunn and consisting of prominent individuals from both the public and private sectors.

The CSIS staff of 190 researchers and support staff focus primarily on three subject areas. First, CSIS addresses the full spectrum of new challenges to national and international security. Second, it maintains resident experts on all of the world's major geographical regions. Third, it is committed to helping to develop new methods of governance for the global age; to this end, CSIS has programs on technology and public policy, international trade and finance, and energy.

Headquartered in Washington, D.C., CSIS is private, bipartisan, and tax-exempt. CSIS does not take specific policy positions; accordingly, all views expressed herein should be understood to be solely those of the author(s).

This publication has been principally supported with funds from the Nuclear Threat Initiative. Its contents represent the views, findings, and opinions of the authors and are not necessarily those of the Nuclear Threat Initiative.

Cover Photo Credit
Globes
©Kenny Johnson/Gettyimages

Library of Congress Cataloging-in-Publication Data

Protecting against the spread of nuclear, biological, and chemical
  weapons : an action agenda for the global partnership / project directors,
  Robert J. Elnhorn, Michèle A. Flournoy.
    p. cm.—(CSIS report)
  Includes bibliographical references.
  Contents: v. 1. Agenda for action—v. 2. The challenges—v. 3.
International responses—v. 4. Russian perspectives and priorities.
  ISBN 0-89206-418-8 (set : alk. paper)—ISBN 0-89206-419-6 (v. 1 : alk. paper)—
ISBN 0-89206-420-X (v. 2 : alk. paper)—ISBN 0-89206-421-8 (v. 3 : alk. paper)—
ISBN 0-89206-422-6 (v. 4 : alk. paper)
  1. Arms control. 2. Weapons of mass destruction.
I. Einhorn, Robert J. II. Flournoy, Michèle A. III. Center for
Strategic and International Studies (Washington, D.C.) IV. Series.
JZ5665.P76 2003
327.1'745—dc21   2002155212

The CSIS Press
Center for Strategic and International Studies
1800 K Street, N.W., Washington, D.C. 20006
Telephone: (202) 887-0200
Fax: (202) 775-3199
E-mail: books@csis.org
Web site: http://www.csis.org/

Contents

List of Tables and Figures

About the Project

Since the end of the Cold War, the United States, Europe, and others have worked with the successor states of the Soviet Union to account for, secure, and dismantle nuclear, biological, and chemical weapons, agents, materials, and infrastructure, as well as to help former weapons scientists and specialists reintegrate into civilian work. In large part, these programs have been successful, but there is much unfinished business.

In June 2002, leaders of the Group of Eight (G-8) nations announced a global partnership against the spread of weapons and materials of mass destruction. In the words of former U.S. senator Sam Nunn, "This global partnership represents a major step in the right direction in terms of how the United States and its partners and allies must work together to prevent dangerous groups from gaining control of the most dangerous materials—materials that could be used to carry out catastrophic terrorism."

The project—Strengthening the Global Partnership: Protecting against the Spread of Nuclear, Biological, and Chemical Weapons—seeks to reinforce and expand upon the objectives of the G-8's Global Partnership against the Spread of Weapons and Materials of Mass Destruction, by advancing support in Europe, Asia, and North America for assistance programs aimed at reducing the threats posed by nuclear, biological, and chemical weapons and materials.

Over the last year, CSIS has led a consortium of 15 influential policy research organizations in Europe, North America, and Asia as part of a three-year project, sponsored by the Nuclear Threat Initiative (NTI), aimed at strengthening future threat reduction efforts. The consortium has concluded a major assessment, published here, that identifies shortfalls and lessons learned from existing threat reduction programs; recommends future programmatic objectives; and proposes how best to accomplish the remaining tasks.

Based on the findings and recommendations of this study, during the second phase of the project, consortium partners will actively reach out to key constituencies—government officials, parliamentarians, journalists, scholars, and other opinion leaders—to promote governmental and public support for the goals outlined by the G-8 in June 2002 and, in particular, to ensure that the Global Partnership's ambitious funding target ($20 billion over 10 years) is met.

This four volume set, entitled *Protecting against the Spread of Nuclear, Biological, and Chemical Weapons: An Action Agenda for the Global Partnership,* is designed to assist the reader in assessing threat reduction programs to date and identifying priorities for the future. The assessment consists of four volumes:

Volume 1: Agenda for Action
Volume 2: The Challenges
Volume 3: International Responses
Volume 4: Russian Perspectives and Priorities

For more information on the project, please visit our Web site at <http://www.csis.org/isp/sgp/index.htm>

Project Partners

Canada—Centre for Security and Defence Studies, Carleton University
European Union—EU Institute for Security Studies
France—Fondation pour la Recherche Stratégique
Germany—Stiftung Wissenschaft und Politik
International—Stockholm International Peace Research Institute
International—International Institute for Strategic Studies
Italy—Landau Network–Centro Volta/Union Scienziati Per Il Disarmo
Japan—Japan Institute of International Affairs
Netherlands—Netherlands Institute of International Relations "Clingendael"
Norway—Norwegian Institute of International Affairs
Russia—PIR Center for Policy Studies in Russia
Russia—Institute of World Economy and International Relations (IMEMO)
Sweden—Swedish Institute of International Affairs
United Kingdom—Centre for Defence Studies, King's College London
United States—Center for Strategic and International Studies

Eliminating the Legacy of the Cold War: Background

After the disintegration of the Soviet Union, Russia, like other newly independent states, faced a number of complex problems brought on by the difficulty of adapting to its new place in the world and by its drastically reduced economic capabilities. Russia's unavoidable transitional crisis period and, of greater importance, its inconsistent budgeting policy raised serious concerns regarding its ability to dismantle its Cold War legacy independently. The matter at hand was to eliminate, in the near future, the vast arsenal of weapons of mass destruction (WMD) and delivery vehicles; to ensure the safe transport and storage of such weapons as well as nuclear weapons materials; to dispose of hundreds of tons of highly enriched uranium and plutonium; and to prevent leaks of knowledge, technology, and materials critical for creating WMD.

Since the early 1990s, a group of developed democratic states, primarily the United States, has been providing Russia with substantial assistance for the elimination of surplus WMD and weapons material inherited from the former USSR as well as for the prevention of the proliferation of these weapons, material, and sensitive information. The donor states consider this assistance an important component for ensuring their own security. It is obvious that after the Cold War ended the proliferation of WMD has been one of the greatest menaces—likely the gravest of threats—to international and national security.

At present, the assistance to Russia for eliminating the Cold War legacy is provided bilaterally by 11 countries. This is also done multilaterally by the European Union (EU) and the European Bank for Reconstruction and Development (EBRD). Official data in the donor states show that from 1992 to 2001 the total funds allocated for this purpose amounted to more than $5 million.[1] This external assistance allowed Russia to resolve key issues associated with the transportation and storage of nuclear weapons materials; start eliminating strategic arms pursuant to the first Strategic Arms Reduction Treaty (START I); and make the first but important steps toward preparing for the elimination of chemical weapons (CW). Assistance has contributed significantly to making the necessary connection between Russia's post–Cold War national security needs and economic capabilities on the one hand, and its vast arsenal of WMD including delivery vehicles and a decaying, giant weapons-industry complex on the other.

At the same time, a decade of international assistance to Russia to solve these problems has brought to light the difficulties—which are partially unavoidable—in

---

1. Dollar amounts refer to U.S. dollars unless stated otherwise.

implementing this assistance. The difficulties relate to the international programs that deal, to a certain extent, with some of the key components of Russia's military machine. The natural interest of the donor states to confirm that the funds provided to Russia are spent in (what the donor states believe is) the proper way is hindered by the fervent desire of Russia's military command and military industry management to protect Russia's national secrets. The difficulties that arise are due by and large to Russia's elite, who do not always fully recognize the interests and motivation of the donor countries—the suspicion and narrow-minded understanding of the interests of the Russian military command and defense industry and often by rent-seeking pursuits by the top echelons.

Continued cooperation with the developed democracies for eliminating the Cold War legacy—a necessary task—requires a careful rethinking of both positive and negative experiences, an evaluation of the scale and nature of the accumulated problems, and the elimination of difficulties that have been revealed.

The Legacy of the Cold War

The defeat of the USSR after its military, political, and ideological confrontations with the West brought upon the newly independent states (NIS) that had emerged from the remains of the Soviet Union the need to solve several large-scale problems associated with the Cold War legacy. These problems existed mainly in Russia, Ukraine, Kazakhstan, and Belarus—where the Soviet strategic forces had been deployed. The difficulties in question are most acute in Russia, however. The attitude of the military was partly responsible, but most of the responsibility lies in the strategy employed by the Soviet leaders when they determined where to build the weapons complexes. The major industrial centers for creating these WMD and delivery systems were located on the territory of the present-day Russian Federation. This was an example of the distrust—carefully hidden but still strong—that the Communist Party of the Soviet Union (CPSU) leaders felt toward the people and the elites of the other Soviet republics.

The above-mentioned problems can be categorized into seven large groups. First, it was necessary within an extremely short time to return to Russia about 3,300 strategic nuclear warheads that were located in Ukraine, Kazakhstan, and Belarus.[2] It was no less important to transfer to Russia the thousands of tactical nuclear warheads deployed during the Cold War in Central and Eastern Europe and on the territories of the NIS, formed after the disintegration of the USSR. In addition, the size of Russia's arsenal—strategic as well as tactical—was rapidly decreasing in the 1990s. Thus, within the past decade, the number of warheads on strategic delivery vehicles has decreased by approximately 1,100 units; and warheads on tactical delivery vehicles have decreased, according to Western sources, by 10,000 to 15,000 warheads. Ten years ago, the former USSR had 15,000 to 20,000

---

2. According to START I accounting rules for strategic nuclear warheads, in 1991, 1,804 warheads in Ukraine were deployed on strategic delivery vehicles; 1,410 were deployed in Kazakhstan; and 81 in Belarus. *SIPRI Yearbook 1994* (Oxford: Oxford University Press, 1994), 288–289.

such weapons. At the beginning of this decade, Russia had 3,500 to 4,000 warheads.[3] In other words, it was necessary, within less than ten years, to relocate about 20,000 nuclear warheads, ensure their secure storage in new storage facilities, eliminate a percentage of them and provide for the secure storage and disposition of highly enriched uranium (HEU) and plutonium, a by-product of the nuclear weapons dismantling process.[4]

In the late 1980s and early 1990s, concerns regarding social disintegration and political and economic chaos on the territory of the former USSR were widespread. If those gloomy forecasts had come true, WMD and weapons material could have gotten into the hands of extremist groups, regional warlords, mafia bosses, and leaders of quasi states appearing on the territory of the former empire. This apocalyptic picture was the main incentive for starting large-scale assistance to Russia to reduce threats associated with WMD and development and production facilities.

Second, in the former USSR, since the early 1990s, a reduction of strategic arms—land-based ballistic missiles and their silos, sea-launched ballistic missiles and nuclear-fuelled ballistic missile submarines, and long-range bombers—has been under way. Between 1991 and 2000, the number of former Soviet strategic delivery vehicles was reduced by 1,300; the reduction was mainly due to the retirement of ballistic missiles.[5] During the coming decade Russia's arsenal will be reduced by about 900–1,000 ballistic missiles and 4,000–4,500 nuclear warheads. The decision to reduce the number of strategic arms has led to a new problem—how to destroy the missiles, their launchers, and the highly toxic missile fuel in an environmentally safe way. More than 150,000 tons of liquid missile fuel (heptyl) and oxidant have to be eliminated. Solving these problems requires a large financial outlay to build missile and fuel elimination facilities as well as to dismantle several thousand strategic nuclear warheads.

Third, it is necessary to dispose of 122 nuclear submarines. Some are kept afloat at naval bases with spent nuclear fuel still on board. Fresh fuel for nuclear

---

3. No official Russian data provide the number of Russian tactical nuclear weapons, but estimates by Russian and foreign experts allow for assessment of the scale of the Russian tactical arsenal. See A. Arbatov, "Reduction of Tactical Nuclear Weapons: From Unilateral Steps to International Commitments," in A. Arbatov et al., *Razoruzhenie i bezopasnost´ 1997–1998: Rossiia i mezhdunarodnaia sistema kontrolia nad vooruzheniiami: razvitie ili raspad* (Disarmament and security, 1997–1998: Russia and the international arms control system: development or decay) (Moscow: Nauka, 1997); Aleksei Arbatov, *Bezopasnost´: rossiiskii vybor* (Security: Russia's choice) (Moscow: EPItsentr, 1999), 471; *SIPRI Yearbook 2001: Armaments, Disarmament and International Security* (Oxford: Oxford University Press, 2001), 466.

4. According to the Russian journalist, Dmitri Litovkin, by the end of 1993, the storage facilities of the 12th Main Directorate of the Ministry of Defense of the Russian Federation had received 17,000 tactical nuclear warheads from Central and Eastern Europe and the former Soviet republics. See Dmitri Litovkin, "Cooperation between the 12th Main Directorate of the Ministry of Defense of the Russian Federation and the U.S. Department of Defense under the Cooperative Threat Reduction Program," in *Cooperative Threat Reduction Program: How Efficient?* ed. Ivan Safranchuk, Study Paper No. 13 (Moscow: PIR Center, January 2000), 13.

5. In September 1990, the Soviet Union had approximately 2,500 strategic delivery vehicles; by July 2001, for the former Soviet Union this number had been reduced to 1,198. "Current Strategic Nuclear Forces of the Former Soviet Union," Fact Sheet, Arms Control Association, October 2001, www.armscontrol.org/assorted/sovforces.asp.

submarines is enriched from 21 percent to 90 percent with regard to the content of uranium 235. This might imply that fuel on board is highly enriched unspent fuel. Many of the submarines have two nuclear reactors. Also requiring a solution is the issue of radioactive waste reprocessing and storage.

Fourth, in the coming decade Russia will have to destroy munitions containing about 40,000 tons of chemical agents as well as the agents themselves. Insufficient financing has allowed only second- and third-category chemical weapons to be destroyed by the summer of 2002.[6]

Fifth, the safe storage and disposition of nuclear weapons material is of the utmost importance. According to Western data, Russia produced 120–150 tons of plutonium and 1,000–1,350 tons of HEU usable for nuclear weapons. U.S. government agencies believe that 603 tons (sometimes the figure of 650 tons is cited) of this amount is "outside" nuclear weapons.[7] There is no confidence that the plutonium and HEU are securely stored, and the possibility of theft cannot be ruled out. Because the availability of weapons-grade nuclear materials is the key factor in the successful implementation of nuclear weapons programs and because such programs are under way today not only in a number of states governed by extremist regimes but, quite possibly, in certain terrorist groups, the proliferation of HEU may raise a special concern. Many experts believe that it is technically much easier to create a relatively primitive nuclear charge with uranium rather than plutonium.

In 1999, Victor Yerastov, an official in the Russia's Ministry of Atomic Energy (MINATOM), emphasized the importance of ensuring the safe and secure storage of nuclear weapons materials when he declared that in 1998, in Chelyabinsk oblast, nuclear material had been stolen. Russian law enforcement authorities were able to stop this criminal activity; had they not, the national security of Russia could have been damaged.[8] Several cases of attempted theft of highly enriched nuclear materials have been known and confirmed by the Russian authorities. These attempts, of course, were intercepted by law enforcement agencies and failed; one may only guess about how many attempts succeeded.

Sixth, nuclear weapons proliferation prevention depends on retarding the brain drain phenomenon and the accompanying illicit transfer of information and technology necessary to create nuclear weapons. Experts, primarily from the West, estimate that in the mid-1990s approximately 60,000 scientists and engineers were

---

6. Category 3 chemical weapons include unfilled munitions, devices, and equipment designed specifically to employ chemical weapons. Category 2 chemical weapons are based on non-schedule 1 chemicals (schedule 1 chemicals are high risk and are rarely used for peaceful purposes); one example of a category 2 chemical is phosgene. See footnote on page 81 for additional information.

7. Official Russian data on stockpiles of nuclear weapons-grade material are unavailable. The amount of such materials not in nuclear warheads may vary: it increases as a result of the withdrawal of weapons-grade material from nuclear weapons being dismantled, but it decreases as this material is disposed. See "Nuclear Nonproliferation: Security of Russia's Nuclear Material Improving; Further Enhancements Needed," Report No. GAO-01-312 (Washington, D.C.: U.S. General Accounting Office, February 28, 2001), 1, www.gao.gov/new.items/d01312.pdf.

8. Victor Yerastov has said that "nuclear malefactors" in Chelyabinsk region were able to seriously damage the state's interests. *Yaderny Kontrol* (in Russian) No. 6 (November–December 1999): 40–42.

involved in the development, design, and delivery of WMD in Russia, with 15,000–18,000 possessing critical knowledge in their areas of expertise.[9]

The end of a tough military and political confrontation with the West and the elimination of Soviet economic management has led to a vast reduction in funding for the Russian military-scientific and military-industrial complexes. The worsening of the social and economic situation in "closed cities," military enterprises, and research centers has created the potential for the proliferation of sensitive information and the possible theft of weapons material.

Seventh, the availability at Russian naval bases in the North and Far East of large stockpiles of CW, nuclear materials, and many retired nuclear submarines with unloaded nuclear reactors may result in ecological mishaps, including environmental contamination of the marine environment.

These seven conditions make it imperative that external assistance to Russia aid in solving three main problems:

■ Prevention of proliferation of WMD and the means to deliver such weapons;

■ Adherence by Russia to its commitments under arms control agreements; and

■ Reduction of the threat of environmental contamination from radioactive waste and chemical agents.

Events of September 11, 2001: The Human Factor

The events of September 11, 2001, highlighted the contours of a new global strategic situation. The signs of a new confrontation are becoming more prominent. Over an extensive area, stretching from the Sahara to the Korean peninsula and from the Hindu Kush to Indonesia, forces are attempting to stop and even reverse the trend toward globalization and modernization; these forces are launching a challenge against developed regions and are attempting to revive an imagined utopian past of traditional lifestyles and religion. For these extremist movements and regimes, the major weapon will most likely be terrorist acts—including those that involve WMD.

This poses the question of how the growing threat of mega-terrorism correlates with Russia's excess WMD, means of delivery, relevant production facilities, and development centers.

Russian experts are confident that the nuclear weapons in storage are reliably protected against external threats. The risk of theft of the more-or-less-noticeable quantities of CW and their transfer outside Russia is minimal. It is hard to imagine a chemical munitions railroad car or truck going from the CW storage facility located deep within Russia to its southern or eastern borders.

Threats involving the so-called human factor represent a more pernicious danger. In Russia there are tens of thousands of scientists and engineers who possess sensitive knowledge. Many now either work part-time or get miserable salaries, especially in the closed cities.[10] Some scientists and engineers—especially the

---

9. Henry D. Sokolski and Thomas Riisager, eds., *Beyond Nunn-Lugar: Curbing the Next Wave of Weapons Proliferation Threats from Russia* (Carlisle, Pa.: Strategic Studies Institute, U.S. Army War College, 2002), 118, 122.

younger generation—are seeking jobs abroad, mainly in the United States, Germany, and Israel. In 1999, 9–14 percent of the population aged 30–49 of one closed city wanted to go abroad for employment. More than 50 percent of them are ready to work for a foreign military industry. Twenty-five to 45 percent of experts living in a "missile city" wanted to have jobs abroad.[11]

Russian open sources do not contain information that any Russian specialists in WMD and their delivery vehicles are now working in any of the "states of concern." No one can be sure, however, that they are not in fact there. Interviews have shown that 30–60 percent of nuclear experts would not work in Iraq, Pakistan, or Libya regardless of what the terms and conditions were; 11–25 percent would not work in China, North Korea, or Iran. Missile experts, however, are less choosy. Some 56 percent of them are ready to work in any state of concern,[12] and they too could significantly speed up the development of WMD programs and delivery vehicles. They also might have the opportunity to sell critically important information located within the Russian scientific and research centers; the information could be transmitted through modern electronic communications systems and networks.

The degradation of the social and economic conditions in the closed cities, at military-industry enterprises—especially nuclear ones—and in research centers could facilitate theft or the illicit transfer of nuclear and biological material. Newly employed personnel at these enterprises and centers generally have lower qualifications; this includes the personnel responsible for the reliable performance of equipment and meeting the established safety and security requirements. People employed in the military industry and in science are now more interested in high salaries than they are in the ideological factors that used to play a greater role in ensuring discipline and safety on the job. This creates more favorable conditions for individuals and entities interested in the illicit acquisition of weapons material, technology, and knowledge.

In Russia, the physical, organizational, and technical safety and security measures regarding WMD and weapons material as well as systems for the protection of information were mainly inherited from the Soviet era when these measures were designed mainly to combat external threats. At the present time and in the future, internal threats may become much more dangerous. An employee with a negative attitude toward an employer or with criminal intent may do greater harm in terms of proliferation than a terrorist group or a squad of commandos that attacks a nuclear materials storage facility or other nuclear facility.

Assistance to Russia in preventing the proliferation of WMD, relevant materials, and technology must therefore be targeted not only at better physical protection

---

10. Gary L. Jones, "Nuclear Nonproliferation: Coordination of U.S. Programs Designed to Reduce the Threat Posed by Weapons of Mass Destruction," statement before the Subcommittee on International Security, Proliferation, and Federal Services, Committee on Governmental Affairs, U.S. Senate, Report No. GAO-02-180T (Washington, D.C.: U.S. General Accounting Office, November 14, 2001), www.gao.gov/new.items/d02180t.pdf.

11. Valentin Tikhonov, *Nuclear-Missile Complex of Russia: Mobility of Personnel and Security*, working paper (text in Russian) (Moscow: Carnegie Moscow Center, 2000), 37–41; 76–78, http://pubs.carnegie.ru/workpapers/2000/wp0100.pdf.

12. Ibid., 40, 78.

but, to a larger extent, also to the improvement of the social and economic conditions in the closed cities and other centers where critically important technology and information are concentrated. Physical security has been the first priority from the very start of foreign assistance to Russia, but improving living and working conditions requires significantly more attention.

In addition, halting electronic transfers of sensitive information to states of concern acquires greater importance. Here, a rather serious issue arises: How can the use of global information networks to spread knowledge about WMD be prevented without violating the human rights insisted on by the developed democracies and without introducing international censorship? Donor countries' police forces and Russia's security services need to cooperate on this.

Russia needs to eliminate the types of weapons and related infrastructure referred to in international arms control agreements such as START I, the Chemical Weapons Convention (CWC), and the Biological Weapons Convention (BWC).[13] The failure to fulfill its obligations under these agreements would be injurious for Russia and would mean the loss of its prestige and international influence. If Russia could not honor its commitments, this would devalue the agreements themselves, as well as arms control as a whole, as an important component of international relations. Devaluing such agreements would legitimize the efforts of states of concern in their attempt to acquire WMD of their own.

The growing threat of terrorism also highlights anew the role of biological weapons, which are exceptionally efficient in terms of affecting a wide civilian population and, of special importance for the goals of terrorists, quickly create panic, chaos, and unrest over large regions. International cooperation aimed at preventing the proliferation of biological weapons therefore acquires a special significance.

Russian Cooperation with Other States

The interaction of Russian agencies with their foreign counterparts to eliminate the legacy of the Cold War is based mainly on three codes of law: the civil code of the Russian Federation, the customs code of the Russian Federation, and the tax code of the Russian Federation. The last incorporates a special regulation (Part II, Article 149, paragraph 19) that governs taxation issues associated with assistance rendered.

In addition, in May 1999, federal law 95-FZ, "On Gratuitous Aid (Assistance) to the Russian Federation and Modifications to and Amendment of Laws of the Russian Federation Concerning Taxes and on Establishing Concessions on Payments to the Governmental Extra-Budgetary Funds with Regard to Gratuitous Aid (Assistance) to the Russian Federation," came into force. The procedure for registering technical aid (assistance) projects and programs, and for issuing certificates confirming that the means, products, activities, and services pertaining to technical aid

---

13. The full title of the CWC is the "Convention on the Prohibition of the Development, Production, Stockpiling and Use of Chemical Weapons and on Their Destruction." The full title of the BWC is the "Convention on the Prohibition of the Development, Production and Stockpiling of Bacteriological (Biological) and Toxin Weapons and on Their Destruction."

Table 1.1. Russian Agencies Responsible for International Threat Reduction Agreements

Lead agency	Agreements for cooperative programs[a]	
	Total	No. of the total that are interagency agreements
MINATOM	25	8
Russian Munitions Agency	7	4
Ministry of Defense	6	3
Ministry of Economic Development and Trade	2	0
Aviation and Space Agency	1	1

Source: Table compiled by authors.

a. As of late 2002, five of these agreements have expired.

(assistance), as well as for control over its targeted use, was approved by Russian Federation governmental decree 1046 on September 17, 1999.

Russia's activities regarding the elimination of CW depend mainly on federal law 76-FZ, "On the Elimination of Chemical Weapons," of May 2, 1997, and the specific action plan was outlined in the federal program, "The Elimination of Chemical Weapons Stockpiles," approved by Russian Federation governmental decree 510, of July 5, 2001.

The approaches that the Russian government agencies pursue regarding these issues of cooperation with other countries in the field of safety and security assurance in the nuclear area are determined, to a large extent, by federal law 170-FZ, "On the Use of Atomic Energy," of November 21, 1995, as well as by the May 21, 1963, Vienna Convention on Civil Liability for Nuclear Damage.

External assistance to Russia for eliminating the Cold War legacy is based on international legal support. Since 1992, Russia has concluded 43 agreements with other states and international organizations. Three more agreements are at the preparatory stage: a bilateral agreement with the United Kingdom, a multilateral agreement with the Barents Euro-Arctic Council, and a trilateral agreement with the United States and Norway.

On the Russian side, the following agencies are responsible for foreign cooperation and agreements (see table 1.1): MINATOM, the Russian Munitions Agency, the Ministry of Defense, the Ministry of Economic Development and Trade, and the Russian Aviation and Space Agency as well as the Federal Nuclear and Radiation Safety Authority of Russia and the State Customs Committee. They coordinate the activities of a large number of other federal entities and regional authorities, to varying degrees, with the cooperative programs with other countries. In turn, the Ministry of Foreign Affairs of the Russian Federation is responsible for preparing international agreements.

The majority of the agreements—26—are devoted to the development of Russian cooperative measures with other countries concerning the disposition of

Table 1.2. CTR Agreements Concluded by the Russian Federation, mid-2002

Country	Type of agreement[a]
Canada	1 intergovernmental agreement
EBRD	1 agreement with the government of the Russian Federation
European Union	1 international and 1 intergovernmental agreement
Finland	1 intergovernmental agreement
France	6 intergovernmental agreements (5 are expired)
Germany	2 intergovernmental and 1 interagency agreement
Italy	2 intergovernmental agreements
Japan	1 intergovernmental agreement
Netherlands	2 intergovernmental agreements
Norway	1 intergovernmental agreement
Sweden	1 intergovernmental agreement
United Kingdom	2 intergovernmental agreements
United States	3 international, 5 intergovernmental, 12 interagency agreements

Source: Table compiled by authors.

a. Two of the agreements do not specify the Russian liaison agency. International agreements are agreements that were signed by the presidents of the countries that are parties to the agreements.

nuclear weapons and nuclear materials, their safe and secure storage, and transportation. The elimination of CW and their production facilities is covered by 10 agreements. Four agreements deal with general security issues related to WMD and one treaty is devoted to the elimination of strategic offensive arms.

The majority of the agreements have been concluded between Russia and the United States (see table 1.2), showing the leading U.S. role in assisting Russia in this area. As of mid-2002, three international, five intergovernmental, and twelve interagency agreements have been signed. The first, signed on June 17, 1992, was the "Agreement between the Russian Federation and the United States of America concerning the Safe and Secure Transportation, Storage and Destruction of Weapons and the Prevention of Weapons Proliferation." This agreement:

■ Laid the legal foundation for U.S.-Russia cooperation;

■ Outlined the cooperative efforts between the two countries in providing assistance to Russia for the elimination, safe and secure storage, and transportation of "nuclear, chemical, and other weapons";

■ Determined the executive agents for the implementation of the agreement; and

■ Resolved issues of taxation and customs duties, privileges and immunities for U.S. governmental officials while staying on the territory of the Russian Federation to carry out activities "in relation to this agreement," and several other legal issues.

Article 13 of this agreement is a fundamental one:

> Upon request, representatives of the Government of the United States of America shall have the right to examine the use of any material, training or other services provided in accordance with this Agreement, if possible at sites of their location or use, and shall have the right to inspect any and all related records or documentation during the period of this Agreement and for 3 years thereafter. These inspections shall be carried out in accordance with procedures to be agreed upon by the Parties.[14]

Because the agreement was to expire at midnight of June 15–16, 1999, it was extended for seven years by a special protocol, which is applied provisionally and will come into force when both sides fulfill all necessary internal procedures. In Russia, this protocol is subject to ratification because the 1992 agreement contains norms and provisions—such as customs and tax exemptions, privileges, and immunities; and exemption from civil liability for damage—other than those provided by Russian legislation.

The majority of the interagency agreements with the United States were concluded by MINATOM. The Russian Ministry of Defense signed two agreements, the Ministry of Economic Development and Trade signed two agreements, and the Agency for Munitions signed one agreement.

As a rule, the preparation of these types of agreements includes working meetings with representatives of all federal executive agencies concerned. During such meetings, the negotiating position of the Russian delegation is decided and draft directives are developed. The directives are then subjected to thorough evaluation by the senior officials of the relevant ministries and agencies and are sent via diplomatic channels to the Russian delegations carrying out corresponding negotiations. Draft directives vetted at the interagency level are approved by a decision of the government of the Russian Federation. Delegations participating in multilateral negotiations are composed of representatives of the Russian Ministry of Foreign Affairs and other concerned federal executive agencies. The composition of delegations is approved by a decree or a directive of the government of the Russian Federation. A Russian Ministry of Foreign Affairs representative is usually the head of the delegation.

This bureaucratic consensus in preparing international agreements is typical in both Russia and abroad. It has both strengths and weaknesses. The process accounts for the positions of all agencies concerned and carefully works through the technical details of the agreements, thus ensuring stability and consistency in the decisionmaking process. It also results in a long preparatory period and, more important, in the domination of the lead agency's interests in the preparation and implementation of the agreement. In Russia, these interests are not always in line with the country's political interests. In addition, the bureaucratic-consensus

---

14. "Appendix C: United States and Russian Agreement on the SSD Program," www.wws.princeton.edu/cgi-bin/byteserv.prl/~ota/disk1/1993/9320/932012.PDF.

approach is not usually efficient when it is necessary to make serious political decisions requiring the rethinking of habitual attitudes and plans.

The weakest point of the Russian mechanism of cooperation with other countries in eliminating the Cold War legacy is the lack of a superagency, a coordinating and controlling body capable of overcoming departmental self-interest. It would be difficult, if not impossible, to overcome such difficulties and implement those programs and projects of great importance to Russia without such a body. However, the lack of such an umbrella agency suits the interests of many Russian entities involved in the area of international cooperation; if such an agency existed they would fear they would lose some of their authority.

U.S. Programs

The United States is largest donor state providing assistance to Russia to reduce threats arising from Soviet WMD. U.S. efforts represent a wide and complex web of programs and projects implemented by the U.S. Departments of Defense, Energy, Commerce, and State. At the beginning of this decade, the U.S. Department of Defense (DOD) was implementing twelve major programs in this area; the U.S. Department of Energy (DOE) had thirteen, and the U.S. Department of State (DOS) had three programs.[15] In addition, the U.S.-Russia intergovernmental agreement constitutes the basis for a large-scale program (the HEU-LEU program) for purchasing Russian uranium from dismantled warheads, which is then used as fuel for U.S. nuclear power plants. This program is a commercial program and is not funded by the U.S. federal budget.

The United States provides Russia with aid for the disposition of CW and strategic offensive arms subject to reduction; the safe and secure transportation, storage, and withdrawal of weapons from combat duty; and help in preventing the proliferation of WMD. The U.S. Congress allocates funds for these programs annually after approval of budget requests submitted by the corresponding U.S. federal agencies. In the United States, as in Russia, there is no one executive body responsible for coordinating the multiple programs and projects regarding assistance to Russia and the other NIS.

THE U.S. LEGISLATIVE FOUNDATION. The terms cooperative threat reduction (CTR) programs and Nunn-Lugar programs (named after the two U.S. senators who initiated them) strictly speaking refer to programs implemented by the DOD. Since the end of the 1990s, DOD has been receiving less than half of the funds that were allocated for these programs. It is also important that each U.S. federal agency is funded under a separate act, and terms and conditions for rendering assistance to the receiving countries under each act is different. For example, requirements in the National Defense Authorization Act, which provides funding for DOD, are not outlined also in the Energy and Water Development Appropriations Act, which determines the budget of the DOE.

The early fall 1991 meeting between Sam Nunn, then chairman of the U.S. Senate Armed Services Committee, and Mikhail Gorbachev, the president of the USSR,

---

15. The number of programs changes from time to time because some of them overlap, others are completed or reach the end of their allotted time period, and new ones appear.

was the start of U.S. assistance for eliminating the Cold War legacy to the NIS of the former USSR. During their discussion, Gorbachev indicated that during the August 1991 coup d'état attempt in the Soviet Union he had not been in control of Soviet nuclear weapons. This led Nunn and his colleague, Senator Richard Lugar, to the alarming conclusion that the disintegration of the USSR had produced a set of entirely new problems, including the possibility that Soviet nuclear weapons might get into the hands of unstable, anti-Western regimes and even terrorist groups.[16]

Guided by such concerns, in November 1991 the U.S. Congress adopted the Soviet Nuclear Threat Reduction Act[17] as an integral part of the Conventional Armed Forces in Europe (CFE) Treaty Implementation Act.[18] This legislation allowed the U.S. president to spend $400 million out of the U.S. Department of Defense budget in FY 1992 to assist "the Soviet Union, its republics and any successors" in the:

- Elimination of nuclear, chemical, and other armaments;

- Transportation, storage, decommissioning, and safeguarding of armaments as relates to elimination;

- Implementation of monitoring measures to prevent the proliferation of such armaments.[19]

This legislation embraced the concept of helping the former USSR, now Russia and other NIS, eliminate the legacy of the Cold War, and it proceeds from the basis that such assistance serves U.S. national security interests. The United States views its assistance as supplementing the efforts of states receiving the assistance but not substituting for them. The assistance conditions oblige the recipient states to commit to:

- Invest their own substantial resources in the dismantling or elimination of armaments;

- Refrain from any programs for the modernization of the armed forces in excess of the legitimate defense needs and from replacing of the WMD being eliminated;

- Refrain from using nuclear weapons material and other components of the nuclear weapons that are being eliminated for the building of new nuclear weapons;

- Assist the United States in verifying the destruction of weapons subject to elimination;

- Follow all corresponding agreements on arms control; and

---

16. *The Nunn-Lugar Vision: 1992–2002* (Washington, D.C.: Nuclear Threat Initiative, 2002), 5, www.nti.org/e_research/nunn-lugar_history.pdf.

17. *Soviet Nuclear Threat Reduction Act of 1991*, Public Law 102-228, November 27, 1991, www.fas.org/nuke/control/ctr/docs/hr3807.html. This act was a part of the CFE Treaty Implementation Act; see note 18.

18. *Conventional Forces in Europe Treaty Implementation Act*, Public Law 102-228, November 27, 1991, www.fas.org/nuke/control/ctr/docs/s3807.html.

19. Ibid., Section 211.

- Respect internationally acknowledged human rights, including minority rights.

In October 1993, the Soviet Nuclear Threat Reduction Act was renamed the Cooperative Threat Reduction Act,[20] and the programs and projects financed under this legislation were renamed cooperative threat reduction programs. In addition, since 1993, the Cooperative Threat Reduction Act has been a part of the U.S. National Defense Authorization Act, which incorporates the above terms and conditions for providing assistance to the recipient countries.

This 1993 legislation expanded the range of tasks to be resolved through CTR programs. Objectives were divided into five major groups: the return of nuclear weapons from the NIS to Russia, the disposition of weapons, the safe and secure storage and transportation of WMD and weapons material, the elimination of CW, and support for demilitarization.

In the 1990s, the list of constraints, terms, and conditions for providing assistance to Russia and other NIS of the former USSR continued to expand. When the federal budget for fiscal year (FY) 1996 was undergoing approval, the U.S. Congress prohibited use of the funds appropriated for CTR programs for peacekeeping operations on the territory of Russia. The U.S. president subsequently had to formally certify that funds appropriated for Russian nuclear scientists were not being used for the upgrading of the Russian strategic forces or research and development (R&D) in the field of weapons of mass destruction. In addition, the U.S. administration was obliged to confirm annually that Russia was strictly following the conventions on chemical and biological weapons.

Since 1998, funds appropriated for the CTR programs cannot be used for the rehabilitation of the environment and the housing and retraining of servicemen or employees of the military industrial complex. The U.S. Congress has made it clear, for example, that taxes paid by U.S. taxpayers should be used to improve housing for U.S. service personnel, not Russians.

The fact that U.S. assistance is conditioned on the fulfillment of certain requirements, especially in the area of U.S. control over the use of the received funds, is a sore spot in Russia-U.S. relations. These conditions are often viewed as an attempt to disarm Russia and limit its freedom of action in the world arena. Such views follow from a poor understanding of the U.S. policymaking process and the concerns of U.S. lawmakers. In turn, however, such misunderstanding is the cause of many of the difficulties faced in the practical implementation of U.S.-Russia cooperative efforts. Thus the implementation of some important programs, primarily concerning the elimination of CW, has faced grave difficulties, caused in part by the lack of preparedness by the Russian public authorities to take into account the terms and conditions tied to U.S. assistance. In spring 2002, the United States suspended funding of CTR programs, saying it could not confirm that Russia fully followed the conventions on chemical and biological weapons.[21]

---

20. *Cooperative Threat Reduction Act of 1993,* Public Law 103-160, November 30, 1993, www.fas.org/nuke/control/ctr/docs/hr2401.html.

21. Judith Miller, "U.S. Warns Russia of Need to Verify Treaty Compliance," *New York Times,* April 8, 2002, A1.

Conceptual framework for ctr assistance. During most of the 1990s, in the first stage of U.S. assistance to the NIS, the West anticipated social and political disintegration, chaos, a deepening of the economic crises in Russia and the NIS, and the possible seizure of power by extremist anti-Western forces. Many experts and politicians believed such developments could lead to the uncontrolled spread of WMD, relevant material, knowledge, and technology beyond the borders of the former USSR. The West therefore tried to foster speedy and secure consolidation of nuclear weapons in reliably guarded storage facilities, ensure the safety of nuclear materials, and eliminate strategic arms.

At the beginning of the twenty-first century, the chance that Russia will somehow disintegrate and fall into political chaos is negligible. The country successfully completed the presidential transition from Boris Yeltsin to Vladimir Putin. The second president of Russia has succeeded in stabilizing the political situation and has implemented a well-balanced and pragmatic foreign policy, cooperating with the West on the majority of key international issues. Since Russia's 1998 financial crisis, the Russian economy, while it cannot be described as flourishing, has emerged from the desperate straits it was in during most of the 1990s.

The September 11, 2001, terrorist acts and the anthrax scare in the United States during the fall of 2001 left no doubt that nuclear and biological mega-terrorism represents a real and aggravating threat to the national security of many countries. Although experts had predicted such a course of events, it was alarming that the analysts' predictions were starting to come true. Since September 2001 there has been an upheaval in the understanding of what constitutes global security.

Today the U.S. assistance programs to Russia, at least conceptually, are tied more than ever to preventing terrorist groups from acquiring WMD. A January 2001 report prepared by a group of U.S. experts, headed by former senator Howard Baker and Lloyd Cutler, an attorney, has increased relevance since September 2001:

1. The most urgent unmet national security threat to the United States today is the danger that weapons of mass destruction or weapons-usable material in Russia could be stolen or sold to terrorists or hostile nation states and used against American troops abroad or citizens at home. . . .

2. Current nonproliferation programs in the Department of Energy, the Department of Defense, and related agencies have achieved impressive results thus far, but their limited mandate and funding fall short of what is required to address adequately the threat.[22]

The concept of a global coalition against mega-terrorism, proposed by Sam Nunn and Richard Lugar early in this decade, should play an important part in the formation of new political frameworks for programs and efforts aimed at preventing the proliferation of WMD. The United States, Russia, and Europe must lead and help guide global efforts and actions targeted at ensuring the safety, transparency,

---

22. Howard Baker and Lloyd Cutler, *A Report Card on the Department of Energy's Nonproliferation Programs with Russia* (Washington, D.C.: Secretary of Energy Advisory Board, U.S. Department of Energy, January 10, 2001), Executive Summary iii, www.eisenhowerinstitute.org/programs/globalpartnerships/safeguarding/threatreduction/BakerCutlerReport.pdf.

accounting, and security of nuclear weapons and nuclear materials not only in the former USSR but all around the world. Wider measures should be taken with regard to biological materials that can be used as weapons. Such measures should include the development of universally binding regulations for the safe conduct of research and handling of hazardous pathogens, cooperation by the special services, the joint development of new medicines.[23]

The global coalition against mega-terrorism features a new role for Russia: Russia acts not only as a country-recipient of U.S. assistance but also as a leading U.S. partner in the global antiterrorist campaign:

> If the USA and Russia start together, as partners, combating terrorism and the threat by weapons of mass destruction, and encourage other states to join in this combat, the world would become a much safer place for our children and grandchildren.[24]

Although President George W. Bush and other U.S. political leaders understand the new conceptual views on the nature of threats to national and international security, the structure and orientation of U.S. assistance programs to Russia are largely unaffected for several reasons. First, there remains the need to continue to implement previously launched programs. The emergence of new threats and hazards does not mean that the previous threats have disappeared or their importance reduced. Also, the programs and projects launched in the 1990s have acquired an institutional and conceptual momentum. Last, the development and implementation of new programs related to the human factor require drastically new ways of thinking on the part of both the donor states and Russia.

FUNDING OF U.S. PROGRAMS. Although the Soviet Nuclear Threat Reduction Act of November 1991 was the first practical step in establishing a multidimensional system of programs and projects of U.S. assistance to Russia, practical interaction between Russia and the United States began only after the presidents of Russia and the United States signed the agreement concerning the safe and secure transportation, storage, and destruction of weapons and prevention of weapons proliferation in June 1992. This umbrella agreement formed the framework for later agreements between U.S. and Russian state agencies to solve specific issues.

The first stages of CTR programs were implemented mainly by DOD. In 1994, however, DOE became involved by implementing two programs of its own. The first, a laboratory-to-laboratory program, was aimed at the safety and security of nuclear materials. The second, the Initiatives for Proliferation Prevention (IPP), was targeted at improving the economic situation in the closed nuclear cities.

In 1995, the U.S. Congress recommended expanding the participation by DOE in assistance programs for Russia. DOE became the conduit for all projects dealing with protection, control, and accounting of nuclear material. At the same time, the State Department was charged with promoting U.S. participation in activities at the International Science and Technology Center (ISTC), which was created in 1992 to

---

23. *The Nunn-Lugar Vision: 1992–2002,* 14–15.
24. Ibid., 15.

Table 1.3. U.S. Funding for CTR through Selected U.S. Government Agencies, 1990–1999, millions of U.S. dollars

U.S. agency	Appropriated by Congress		Obligated		Disbursed	
	NIS (including Russia)	Russia only	NIS (including Russia)	Russia only	NIS (including Russia)	Russia only
DOD	2,711.9	1,674.8	2,137.9	1,224.5	1,572.3	790.0
DOE	1,302.6	1,023.8	1,073.8	839.4	868.0	683.6
DOS	99.2	48.1	99.2	48.1	93.0	46.7
Total	4,113.7	2,746.7	3,308.9	2,112.0	2,533.3	1,520.4

Source: Office of the Coordinator of U.S. Assistance to the NIS, "U.S. Government Assistance to and Cooperative Activities with the NIS of the FSU: FY 1999 Annual Report" (Washington, D.C.: U.S. Department of State, January 2000).

identify scientists from the former USSR countries who had been engaged in military R&D and retrain them for civilian projects.[25]

In 1996, at the initiative of three senators—Domenici, Lugar, and Nunn—financing for the assistance programs to Russia was enlarged and the role of DOE expanded. In addition, several new areas for assistance were approved. They included projects as varied as assisting Russia in disposing spent nuclear fuel from submarines to decommissioning plutonium production reactors. Additional attention was paid to efforts to ensure the safety and security of weapons materials in Russia and the NIS. This, in particular, resulted in a significant increase in the financing of the nuclear materials protection, control, and accounting program.

On the whole, during the past decade the U.S. Congress has appropriated more than $4 billion for assistance to the NIS. During the first eight years of the assistance programs, the Russian share was approximately 67 percent of all appropriated funds, 64 percent of the total costs of concluded contracts, and 60 percent of the total amount of the paid contracts. As the 1990s progressed, Russia's share increased. Russia is now allocated about 75 percent of all corresponding appropriations, mainly owing to completion of programs in Ukraine and Kazakhstan.

Not all of the funds appropriated by Congress in the 1990s were disbursed (see table 1.3); about $775 million remains obligated but not disbursed, and the Russian share of that amounts to just under $600 million. This is explained mainly by long time lags between the appropriation and concluding the agreements between the Russian and the U.S. agencies on the details of the programs and projects. This rests as much on bureaucratic foot dragging as on the real difficulties of generating joint decisions regarding U.S.-Russia cooperation.

In the 1990s, the main areas of U.S. assistance to Russia for eliminating the legacy of the Cold War were assistance in eliminating strategic arms; ensuring the safe

---

25. "Russia: International Science and Technology Center (ISTC)," Newly Independent States Nuclear Profiles database, www.nti.org/db/nisprofs/russia/forasst/otherusg/istc.htm.

Table 1.4. U.S. Allocations for Threat Reduction Programs in Russia, FY 1992–FY 2000; share of program allocations

Type of program	U.S. agency	Percent of allocations
Delivery vehicles	DOD	28
Nuclear safety and security	DOD	22
Materials protection, control, and accounting	DOE	15

Source: Harold J. Johnson, "Weapons of Mass Destruction: U.S. Efforts to Reduce Threats from the Former Soviet Union," testimony before the Subcommittee on Emerging Threats and Capabilities, U.S. Senate Committee on Armed Services, Report No. GAO/T-NSIAD/RCED-00-119 (Washington, D.C.: U.S. General Accounting Office, March 6, 2000), 13, www.gao.gov/new.items/n500119t.pdf.

and secure storage and transport of nuclear weapons; and physical protection, control, and accounting of nuclear materials (see table 1.4). More than two-thirds of all funds appropriated for assistance to Russia were spent to implement these programs.

Russia's financial crisis of 1998, the realization that a change in Russia's top political leadership was unavoidable, and the growing activity of militarist and leftist forces in Russia raised serious concerns in the West. The fear that a chaotic course of events could lead to unpredictable consequences grew as well.

President Bill Clinton therefore decided to increase significantly the financing for assistance programs to Russia. His proposals, outlined in his January 1999 annual State of the Union Address, were presented as the Expanded Threat Reduction Initiative, and could cost, according to Clinton administration estimates, about $4.5 billion over six years. DOD's CTR programs would account for $2.8 billion of that.[26] In addition, President Clinton promised to lobby for significant increases for European and Japanese assistance to Russia. The U.S. Congress almost doubled the financing for these U.S. efforts, but it did not agree with the president's proposal to appropriate the requested funds in full.

The U.S. administration's efforts to motivate other developed democratic states to increase their assistance to Russia did not come to fruition until the June 2002 G-8 summit, when G-8 members agreed to increase the amount of assistance to Russia up to $2 billion a year, noting that it is extremely important that such aid be transformed into concrete decisions, programs, and projects. This may require long-term efforts.

Since the early 1990s, approximately two-thirds of the U.S. funds have been distributed by DOD. Since 2000, however, the role of the DOE has increased significantly (see table 1.5). In terms of amounts of funding, it has approached the same level as DOD for FY 2002, thus almost doubling funding for programs in Russia compared with the 1990s.

26. "Russia: Expanded Threat Reduction Initiative Overview," Nuclear Threat Initiative, nti.org/db/nisprofs/russia/forasst/etri.html.

Table 1.5. U.S. Funding of Security Assistance Programs to the NIS, including additional appropriations, FY 2000–FY 2003, millions of U.S. dollars

U.S. agency	FY 2000		FY 2001		FY 2002		FY 2003
	Request	Allocated	Request	Allocated	Request	Allocated	Request
DOD	484.9	467.1	469.2	443.4	417.6	403.0	428.3
DOE	264.3	238.2	363.4	311.5	229.3	417.6	419.7
DOS	250.5	184.5	141.0	135.1	112.0	184.9	108.9
Total	999.7	889.8	973.6	890.0	759.6	1,005.5	956.9

Sources: *National Defense Authorization Act for FY 2000,* Public Law 106-65; *National Defense Authorization Act for FY 2001,* Public Law 106-398; *National Defense Authorization Act for FY 2002,* Public Law 107-107; William Hoehn, "The Clinton Administration's Fiscal Year 2001 Budget Requests for Nuclear Security Cooperation with Russia" (Washington, D.C.: Russian-American Nuclear Security Advisory Council [RANSAC], March 13, 2000); Hoehn, "Analysis of the Bush Administration's Fiscal Year 2002 Budget Requests for U.S.-Former Soviet Union Nuclear Security: Department of Energy Programs" (Washington, D.C.: RANSAC, April 18, 2001); William Hoehn, "Analysis of the Bush Administration's Fiscal Year 2003 Budget Requests for U.S.-Former Soviet Union Nonproliferation Programs" (Washington, D.C.: RANSAC, April 2002), www.ransac.org/new-web-site/related/congress/status/fy2003doe_0402.html.

In March 2001, shortly after the George W. Bush administration came to office in Washington, the administration announced the initiation of studies of the assistance programs to the NIS and of their usefulness for the United States. The Bush administration also announced a reduction in the budget for these programs. Thus, the April 2001 draft of the FY 2002 budget envisaged a reduction in financing for these programs in the amount of $130 million compared with the amount allocated for 2001. The major cuts were at the expense of DOE programs. However, the Congress not only reinstated the total amount allocated for FY 2001 but also increased it by more than $100 million. Most of the additional funds were appropriated by Congress after September 11, 2001, and were intended to enhance efforts to ensure the accounting and security of nuclear materials, the strengthening of export controls, and the reorienting of defense sector scientists to civilian research. Fiscal year 2002 was the first time that more than $1 billion was appropriated for the programs under discussion.

In December 2001, the Bush administration completed its study of assistance programs to the NIS and announced that well-operated and well-managed programs would be given priority. It recommended expanding the financing for four programs:

■ Protection, control, and accounting of nuclear materials, carried out by DOE;

■ Transparency of nuclear weapons and nuclear weapons materials, carried out by DOE;

■ Activities of the ISTC, carried out by DOS; and

- Reorientation of scientists involved in biotechnology research to peaceful purposes, carried out be DOE.

In addition, DOD was given the task of speeding up the construction of a CW elimination facility in the town of Shchuch'ye but was not provided additional funding.

At the same time, the State Department and DOE were charged with exploring alternative, less costly, and more efficient options for disposing of weapons-grade plutonium in Russia. The U.S. administration therefore confirmed its intent to fulfill the U.S.-Russia agreement concerning the disposition of the excess plutonium.

A decision was also made to effect some organizational changes. The program targeted to stop weapons-grade plutonium production in Russia was handed from DOD to DOE. The Nuclear Cities Initiative (NCI) merged with the IPP program, and the Second Line of Defense (SLD) program—targeted to improve the technical capabilities of the Russian customs service to prevent the illicit trafficking of nuclear materials—merged with the Materials Protection, Control, and Accounting (MPC&A) program.[27]

On December 11, 2001, while describing the current position of the United States regarding assistance to Russia, President George W. Bush stressed:

> Acting together we must prevent the most dangerous technologies from getting in the hands of the most dangerous people in the world. Here, our most important partner is Russia, the country we are assisting to dismantle strategic arms, reduce the amount of nuclear materials and strengthen safety and security in nuclear cities. Our two countries will be building up their efforts to expand the civil employment of the scientists who formerly worked for the Soviet military programs. The United States, jointly with Russia, will work on the construction of a nerve agent elimination facility. I will be asking an increase in financing for these vitally important efforts.[28]

However, the Bush administration requested only $957 million for FY 2003 to implement these programs, somewhat less than the amount appropriated for FY 2002.

In addition, the U.S. administration made more rigorous the requirements Russia had to meet for obtaining assistance. In spring 2002, the White House did not confirm to Congress that Russia had fulfilled all requirements under the Common Threat Reduction Act. The matter in hand primarily concerned Russian fulfillment of the CWC and the BWC, the Russian release of all necessary (according to the U.S. stipulations) information, and inspection of the programs. The DOD's allocations to Russia were frozen in spring 2002.

DESCRIPTIONS OF MAJOR U.S. PROGRAMS. The U.S. Department of Defense assists Russia in several main areas. The first is the elimination of strategic arms. Programs include assisting in the transport and elimination of liquid missile fuel;

---

27. "Fact Sheet: Nonproliferation, Threat Reduction Assistance to Russia," Office of the Press Secretary, The White House (Crawford, Texas), December 27, 2001, http://usinfo.state.gov/topical/pol/arms/stories/01122701.htm.

28. Ibid.

Table 1.6. DOD Funding for CTR Programs in Russia, FY 1998–FY 2002, millions of U.S. dollars (in current prices)

Programs	FY 1998	FY 1999	FY 2000	FY 2001	FY 2002
Elimination of strategic arms	77.9	142.4	177.3	177.8	133.4
Dismantling of warheads	—	9.4	9.3	9.3	—
Safe and secure transportation of nuclear weapons	—	10.3	15.2	14.0	9.5
Safe and secure storage of nuclear weapons	36.0	41.7	99.0	89.7	56.0
Storage of fissile materials	57.7	60.9	64.5	57.4	—
Containers for fissile materials	7.0	—	—	—	—
Halting of weapons-grade plutonium production	41.0	29.8	32.3	32.1	41.7
Elimination of chemical weapons	55.4	88.4	20.0	—	50.0
Biological weapons proliferation prevention	—	2.0	12.0	12.0	17.0
Other	22.5	8.0	4.1	22.0	31.8
Total	297.5	392.9	422.7	414.3	339.4

Sources: National Defense Authorization Acts for FY 1998, FY 1999, FY 2000, FY 2001, and FY 2002.

and the elimination of ballistic missile sea launchers, nuclear ballistic missile submarines themselves, intercontinental ballistic missile silos and their missiles, and long-range bombers. The second area encompasses programs ensuring the safe and secure transport and storage of nuclear weapons. The third is for assistance in constructing a nuclear weapons material storage facility at the Production Association Mayak (PO Mayak) site, including supplying containers for these materials. The fourth area is the halting of plutonium production at reactors located in Seversk and Zheleznogorsk. The fifth is the elimination of CW. The sixth area refers to the prevention of biological weapons proliferation. For allocations to these and other programs by DOD, see table 1.6.

To ensure the safe and secure transport of Russian nuclear warheads from their deployment locations and storage facilities to the dismantling enterprises, the DOD has provided the Russian Ministry of Defense with railcars specially equipped to meet enhanced safety requirements, packaging materials, and supercontainers to transport and store the warheads.

DOD also is responsible for the main programs for the storage of Russian nuclear weapons. The construction of the fissile material storage facility at the PO Mayak site is one of the most important CTR programs. When construction of the second phase of the storage facility is completed—it was scheduled for February 2002—the facility will store fissile materials removed from more than 6,000 dis-

Table 1.7. DOE Funding for Assistance Programs in Russia, FY 1992–FY 2002, millions of U.S. dollars (in current prices)

Programs	1992–2000	2000	2001	2002
MPC&A	478.0	139.0	170.0	292.0
NCI	15.0	7.5	27.0	20.0
IPP	140.0	30.0	22.0	34.0
Disposition of weapons-grade plutonium	—	30.0	57.0	42.0
Other	74.0	—	15.0	22.0
Total	707.0	206.5	291.0	410.0

Sources: Amy F. Woolf, "Nuclear Weapons in Russia: Safety, Security, and Control Issues," CRS Issue Brief for Congress, IB98038 (Washington, D.C.: Congressional Research Service, Library of Congress, April 12, 2002), www.fas.org/spp/starwars/crs/IB98038.pdf; "Preliminary Report: Anticipated FY 2003 Budget Request for Department of Energy Cooperative Nuclear Security Programs in Russia" (Washington, D.C.: RANSAC, January 9, 2002); Marsh et al., "Accomplishments of Selected Threat Reduction Programs," May 2001, www.ransac.org/new-web-site/fastfacts/programs_accomplish_rev4.html; Jon B. Wolfsthal et al., eds., *Nuclear Status Report: Nuclear Weapons, Fissile Material, and Export Controls in the Former Soviet Union,* No. 6 (Washington, D.C.: Carnegie Endowment for International Peace, and Monterey, Calif.: Monterey Institute for International Studies, 2001), 3, http://cns.miis.edu/pubs/print/pdfs/nsr/status.pdf.

mantled nuclear warheads. When fully completed, the storage facility will house 25,000 fissile material containers from approximately 12,500 dismantled nuclear warheads.

DOE is currently assisting Russia in three major areas for the prevention of proliferation of nuclear materials, weapon components, and nuclear information/technology (table 1.7). The first area is the protection, control, and accounting of nuclear materials. The second area deals with the disposition of weapons-grade plutonium. The third is targeted to improving the social and economic situation in the closed cities of MINATOM, including preventing brain drain by creating alternative jobs for scientists who were previously engaged in weapons programs.

Materials protection program goals include the safe and secure storage of approximately 603 metric tons of Russian weapons-grade uranium and plutonium.[29] The programs are under way at civilian and military facilities and storage facilities all over Russia. This is the largest program implemented by DOE in Russia. Upgrades of the physical protection systems were done at 21 percent of the Russian storage facilities for HEU that has been removed from dismantled nuclear warheads. Upgrades have begun at storage facilities that house the other two-thirds of such materials. Rapid upgrades have been carried out to improve protection systems at nearly half of the facilities containing such materials.[30]

---

29. "Nuclear Nonproliferation: Security of Russia's Nuclear Material Improving; Further Enhancements Needed," Report No. GAO-01-312.

Table 1.8. Funding for the ISTC, as of November 2002

Country or organization	Financing (%)
United States	35.6
European Union	26.9
Japan	11.7
South Korea	0.4
Norway	0.4
Partners/Others	25.0

Source: ISTC Database Graphs and Tables, International Science and Technology Center, Moscow, Russia, www.istc.ru/istc/website.nsf/fm/z12+Graphs.

The agreement between Russia and the United States regarding the conversion of excess weapons-grade plutonium into forms not usable for weapons, which was signed in September 2000, is of great importance. With the help of DOE, this program will facilitate the ultimate disposition of 34 metric tons of excess weapons-grade plutonium presently located in Russia.

Other programs implemented by DOE—the NCI and the IPP—envisage the creation of alternative jobs for scientists and engineers now employed in the weapons sector as well as the support of commercial partnership projects. DOE also participates in the development of the SLD, which allows for more efficient export control and the prevention of illicit trafficking of nuclear materials.

In Russia, the major U.S. Department of State program for assisting in the elimination of the legacy of the Cold War is the financing and operational support provided to the ISTC in Moscow. The United States is the largest financial contributor, providing about 36 percent of the center's budget (table 1.8).

Since its creation in 1992 through October 2002, the ISTC has supported 1,688 projects carried out in various Russian research institutes. Its main objective is to aid scientists engaged in military research and activities to divert their efforts to civilian tasks and thus prevent the proliferation of WMD and missile technology. Total expenditures by the center for these purposes have been $481 million.[31]

In addition, the State Department participates in events and programs to improve export controls in the NIS and to prevent the illicit trafficking of weapons, weapon materials, and technology beyond national borders.

30. Greg Marsh, Terry Stevens, and Kelly Turner, "Accomplishments of Selected Threat Reduction Programs in Russia, By Agency," Russian-American Nuclear Security Advisory Council (RANSAC), May 2001, www.ransac.org/new-web-site/fastfacts/programs_accomplish_rev4.html. There are other assessments of the quantity of weapons materials covered by protective measures under the MPC&A program; see chapter 3 on page 51.

31. ISTC Database Graphs and Tables, International Science and Technology Center, Moscow, Russia, www.istc.ru/istc/website.nsf/fm/z12+Graphs.

Table 1.9. CTR Aid to Russia from European Countries, Selected Asian Countries, and Canada, 2001–2002, millions of U.S. dollars

Country	Approximate amounts
Japan	350.0
United Kingdom	177.0
European Union	145–148.0
Norway	68.0
France	60.0–70.0
Germany	55.0
Netherlands	14.0
Italy	13.5
Sweden	10.0–15.0
Canada	3.7
Finland	3.7
South Korea	2.7
Total	902.6–920.6

Source: Data compiled by the SCTR project at CSIS, 2002.

European, Asian, and Canadian Programs

The financial support of developed democratic states other than the United States for Russian efforts to eliminate the legacy of the Cold War has not been as large as the U.S. contribution (table 1.9). From 1992 through 2001, other countries provided approximately $920–$930 million if the late 2001 appropriation from the United Kingdom—£83 million—is included.[32] Therefore, to realize the June 2002 G-8 summit pledge to allocate $20 billion for these purposes over the next decade, it would be necessary to increase by about 10 times the annual contributions of the European countries and Japan.

Assistance to Russia by European countries and Japan is less than from the United States because most European assistance is rendered on a two-tier basis, and the economic capabilities of even the largest of European countries are significantly less than those of the United States. Also, each G-8 state allocates funds according to its own interests and ideas about what actual or potential threats must be neutralized first.

Like the United States, other developed democratic states attach great significance to reorientating the Russian military and scientific complex to peaceful

---

32. It is difficult to make accurate estimates owing to differences in the systems of accounting and finance in the countries and the complex administrative and institutional structure of the programs.

Table 1.10. EU Assistance to Russia for CTR Programs, 1992–2001 data, millions of euros

Programs	Funding
ISTC	115.0
Safety, control, and accounting of nuclear materials	23.0
Elimination of chemical weapons	18.5
Disposition of weapons-grade plutonium	5.6
Total	162.1

Source: Kathrin Höhl et al., "European Union," in Robert Einhorn and Michèle Flournoy, project directors, *Protecting against the Spread of Nuclear, Biological, and Chemical Weapons*, Volume 3: *International Responses* (Washington, D.C.: CSIS, 2003).

purposes and providing these scientists with civilian jobs. Consequently, substantial funds—about $150 million—were allocated for the ISTC.

Early on, France, the UK, and Italy assisted Russia in the safe and secure transport and storage of nuclear warheads. As this became less urgent, nuclear safety as a whole, assistance in eliminating CW, and the disposition of weapons-grade plutonium became more prominent. Environmental consequences of potential nuclear and chemical accidents in Russia, including those involving nuclear and chemical weapons, are often perceived in Europe as more dangerous threats than those related to the proliferation of WMD. Therefore, programs related to safety improvements at Russian nuclear reactors may be considered analogous to the U.S. programs to control the proliferation of WMD and delivery vehicles.

THE EUROPEAN UNION. The total contribution by the EU for 1992–2001 to assist Russia in eliminating its Cold War legacy is estimated (without taking account bilateral programs carried out by individual EU members) to be about €162 million (table 1.10), which currently equals about $145–$148 million.[33] All corresponding programs and projects are carried out through the Technical Assistance in the Commonwealth of Independent States (TACIS) program. About two-thirds of the funds allocated by the EU were spent for the ISTC. Other funds were divided among 14 programs that break down into three main groups: safety, control, and accounting for nuclear materials; disposition of weapons-grade plutonium; and the elimination of CW. Funds allocated for the latter programs amount to a comparatively small sum—approximately 7–8 percent of the total amount of assistance provided through the TACIS program.

The EU's recent approach to the issue is determined by regulations it adopted in late 1999. Thus, the EU in its general strategy regarding Russia as adopted in 1999 mentioned the EU Council of Ministers' intent to:

---

33. Kathrin Höhl et al., "European Union," in Robert Einhorn and Michèle Flournoy, project directors, *Protecting against the Spread of Nuclear, Biological, and Chemical Weapons*, Volume 3: *International Responses* (Washington, D.C.: CSIS, 2003).

Table 1.11. EU-Supported Projects, not including the ISTC, July 2001, millions of euros

Project mission	Allocation
Infrastructure to eliminate nerve agents stored in the town of Shchuch'ye	2
Research and experiments regarding demonstration and licensing of mixed-oxide (MOX) fuel	1.5; in addition to 1.3 appropriated in the 1999–2000 budgets
Support for Gosatomnadzor to develop regulatory foundation and documents for disposition of weapons-grade plutonium	1.3
Support for Russian Munitions Agency to fulfill Russian Federation commitments under the CWC	0.8
Joint studies of immobilization techniques for Russian waste containing weapons-grade plutonium	0.4

Source: "Council Joint Action of 17 December 1999 establishing a European Union Cooperation Programme for Non-proliferation and Disarmament in the Russian Federation," Document No. 1999/878/CFSP, December 17, 1999, Articles 2, 4, www.bits.de/EURA/CJA171299.pdf, as implemented by 2001/493/CFSP, June 25, 2001, www.eur.ru/eng/neweur/rae/attach/council_decision.pdf.

— consider developing a consultation mechanism, in addition to existing troika expert level talks, with Russia, possibly involving third countries, on non-proliferation issues, as well as intensifying efforts, including through increased coordination/joint activities with third countries, in support of Russia's CW destruction;

— examine the scope for Joint Actions and Common Positions concerning the safe management of biological, and chemical materials, as well as fissile materials in Russia under IAEA [International Atomic Energy Agency] verification which are designated as no longer necessary for defence purposes, notably on the basis of international conventions. Particular consideration will be given to the International Science and Technology Centre in Moscow.[34]

On December 17, 1999, the EU Council of Ministers established the European Union Nonproliferation and Disarmament Cooperation Program in the Russian Federation to strengthen the EU's role in reducing risks in Russia. One goal is to facilitate better coordination and prevent the duplication of programs by the EU, by individual EU member states, and by states not belonging to the EU. The first stage of the EU program would include the construction of a pilot facility in Gorny for the elimination of CW and would carry out a series of theoretical and experimental

---

34. *Presidency Conclusions, Cologne European Council, 3 and 4 June 1999,* SN 150/99, p. 61, http://europa.eu.int/comm/tfan/varia/koln.pdf.

research projects on the transportation, storage, and disposition of plutonium. Funding allocated in 1999 and 2000 for this work was €8.9 million.[35]

In June 2001, the European Council adopted a decision regarding implementation of the Joint Action Plan as its contribution to the European Union Nonproliferation and Disarmament Cooperation Program in the Russian Federation. A description of five projects to be implemented by June 2003 in Russia with EU support can be seen in table 1.11.

FRANCE. French programs to assist Russia were started in 1992 when the first Russian-French intergovernmental agreement concerning cooperation to eliminate and ensure the security of nuclear weapons as well as the peaceful uses of weapons-grade materials was signed.[36] Eventually several other bilateral agreements were concluded that helped determine the goals, principles, and mechanisms for related cooperation between Russia and France.

From 1992 to 1996, this cooperation included supplying Russia with 100 special containers for the safe transport of nuclear weapons, high-precision tools for dismantling nuclear warheads, and instruments for radiation monitoring of Russian nuclear facilities' personnel and territory. In addition, French assistance was used for construction of a building for the storage of nuclear weapons components near Novosibirsk and for a preliminary study of the possibility of using plutonium as fuel for nuclear reactors. In 1998, Russia, France, and Germany signed a trilateral intergovernmental agreement for a joint research program to study the possibility of modifying Russian reactors to use plutonium mixed-oxide (MOX) fuel. About F460 million—approximately $60–$70 million—was appropriated for these programs. In September 2000, the French government announced its readiness to continue assistance programs in Russia, primarily in the area of using plutonium as fuel for nuclear reactors. It would keep its funding steady.[37]

UNITED KINGDOM. The United Kingdom assists Russia through bilateral as well as multilateral projects. In 1992–1994, 250 special containers and 20 armored vehicles (worth about £35 million) for the transport of nuclear weapons were delivered to Russia. Until 1999, however, most British assistance to Russia involved workshops on the safety of nuclear facilities and supplying the Federal Nuclear and Radiation Safety Authority (Gosatomnadzor), including to PO Mayak, with small shipments of personal computers and other equipment.[38]

---

35. "Council Joint Action of 17 December 1999 establishing a European Union Cooperation Programme for Non-proliferation and Disarmament in the Russian Federation," document no. 1999/878/CFSP, December 17, 1999, Articles 2, 4, www.bits.de/EURA/CJA171299.pdf.

36. On November 12, 1992, France and Russia signed a framework agreement on aid in dismantling Russian nuclear weapons (AIDA) (Accord entre Le Gouvernement de La République Française et Le Gouvernement de La Fédération de Russe sur la coopération dans les domaines de l'élimination, dans des conditions de sécurité, des armes nucléaires en Russie et de l'utilisation a des fins civiles des matières nucléaires issues des armes, signe a Paris le 12 novembre 1992).

37. See Isabelle Facon et al., "France," in Einhorn and Flournoy, Protecting against the Spread of Nuclear, Biological, and Chemical Weapons, Volume 3: International Responses.

38. This does not take into account expenditures incurred by financing safety measures for nuclear reactors in the former USSR. In 1993–1998, the UK allocated £18.25 million through the EBRD.

Table 1.12. German Assistance to Russia, 1993–2002, millions of euros

Types of assistance	Allocation
Construction of the CW elimination facility in Gorny	40.00
Safety, security, and destruction of nuclear weapons	12.50
Trilateral plutonium disposition project	7.00
Ensuring safety at PO Mayak	2.25
Construction of the CW elimination facility in Shchuch'ye	1.50
Total	63.25

Source: Klaus Arnhold, "Germany," in Einhorn and Flournoy, *Protecting against the Spread of Nuclear, Biological, and Chemical Weapons,* Volume 3: *International Responses.*

In June 2000, the United Kingdom completed an interdepartmental review of assistance to the NIS. Also a special nuclear safety fund in the former USSR countries was set up[39] with funding totaling £83.8 million (about $120 million) for 2001–2004. For FY 2001–2004, a total of £70 million will be set aside for weapons-grade plutonium disposition projects, which are expected to last 10 years. In addition, in 2001, the UK reached an agreement with Russia to allocate £12 million (about $18 million) to build a CW elimination facility in Shchuch'ye.[40]

GERMANY. Germany (see table 1.12) has mainly assisted with eliminating excess stockpiles of WMD and delivery vehicles and ensuring the safety and security of nuclear materials. For example, Germany has helped to construct a CW elimination facility in the town of Gorny; it is being constructed on the basis of an October 22, 1993, agreement between the Russian Munitions Agency and the German Ministry of Foreign Affairs. Funds were also allocated for the implementation of the tripartite Russia-Germany-France project on the disposition of weapons-grade plutonium and the safety and security of nuclear materials. Since 2002, funds have been allocated for the building of a CW elimination facility in Shchuch'ye. The funds are allocated annually by the government of Germany through the diplomatic mechanism of the *note verbale,* considered to carry the same weight as intergovernmental agreements.

NORWAY. Norwegian assistance to Russia is based on Norway's Plan of Action for Nuclear Safety Issues, adopted in 1995,[41] to reduce the threat of environmental pollution, primarily aquatic, caused by radioactive waste (RW) and chemical agents.[42] Norway's plan covers:

39. "Cross-Departmental Review of Nuclear Safety in the Former Soviet Union," Spending Review 2000, www.archive.official-documents.co.uk/document/cm48/4807/chap37.html.

40. Paul Cornish, "United Kingdom," in Einhorn and Flournoy, *Protecting against the Spread of Nuclear, Biological, and Chemical Weapons,* Volume 3: *International Responses.*

41. See "The seminar on Nuclear Safety in Severodvinsk," September 10, 1999, http://odin.dep.no/odinarkiv/norsk/dep/ud/1999/taler/032005-090030/index-dok000-n-f-a.html.

42. The Norwegians are aware that there is an undeclared CW storage facility in Russia near the Norwegian border.

- Safety and security of nuclear facilities;

- Management of RW and spent nuclear fuel, their storage, and disposal;

- Prevention of radioactive contamination in the northern regions; and

- Prevention of damage to the environment from military activities.

As of March 2002, Norway had allocated NKr590 million (about $68 million) to implement the above plan. More than 75 percent was for ensuring nuclear safety and the disposal of nuclear fuel and RW.[43] In December 2001 and March 2002, two Norway-UK memorandums of understanding were signed in which Norway committed itself to allocating NKr18.2 million (about $2.1 million) as its contribution for the construction of some of the elements of the power supply system at the CW elimination facility in Shchuch'ye.

ITALY. In 1993, Russia and Italy signed an agreement in which the Italian government provided Russia with specialized equipment designed to ensure the safety of nuclear weapons. The program, with a total cost about $5.5 million, was completed in 1999. In January 2000, a Russian-Italian framework agreement concerning assistance in the implementation of CW elimination in Russia was signed. In this agreement, Italy committed to allocating Lit15 billion (about $8 million) to construct some of the elements of the power supply system for the CW elimination facility in Shchuch'ye as well as provide for the entire town's sanitary and environmental protection equipment.

SWEDEN. In the past ten years, Sweden has spent roughly $10–$15 million to fund assistance programs to countries of the former USSR. About $6 million was spent to implement approximately 100 projects for the safe handling of spent nuclear fuel, especially in Ukraine and Kazakhstan. The largest of Sweden's assistance programs to Russia—at approximately $4 million over the past decade—helps finance the ISTC.[44]

NETHERLANDS. After signing an agreement on December 22, 1998, the Netherlands appropriated f.25 million (about $12 million) to construct the power supply system for the CW elimination facility in Gorny.[45] In addition, about $2 million was to be used for the nuclear materials storage facility at PO Mayak.

FINLAND. Like other Nordic countries, Finland is primarily concerned with the safety of the Russian nuclear reactors near the Finnish border and with the hazards associated with Russian CW. Finland's Radiation and Nuclear Safety Agency has allocated €2.7 million to improve safety systems at the Leningrad and Kola nuclear power plants. Under a separate agreement of October 25, 2000, Finland committed to allocating $1.2 million to furnish chemical agent leak detection systems for the CW storage facility in the town of Kambarka.[46]

---

43. Morten Bremer Mærli, "Norway," in Einhorn and Flournoy, *Protecting against the Spread of Nuclear, Biological, and Chemical Weapons*, Volume 3: *International Responses*.

44. Tor Larsson, "Sweden," in Einhorn and Flournoy, *Protecting against the Spread of Nuclear, Biological, and Chemical Weapons*, Volume 3: *International Responses*.

45. "Financial Assistance of States Donors to the Russian CW Destruction Programme," Russian Munitions Agency, International Cooperation, www.munition.gov.ru/eng/inter.html.

JAPAN. For these kinds of projects, Japan is the second largest donor country to Russia after the United States. In April 1993 the Japanese government decided to allocate $100 million to the NIS to assist in eliminating nuclear weapons; $70 million was intended for Russia. These funds were spent for the construction of a liquid radioactive waste (LRW) reprocessing facility with a processing capacity of about 7,000 cubic meters a year, and for assisting Russia in the disposition of nuclear submarines in the Far East. In June 1999 Keizo Obuchi, the Japanese prime minister, announced the appropriation of an additional $200 million to implement similar new projects. Japan has also allocated about $52 million for financing the ISTC in Moscow.[47]

SOUTH KOREA. Since 1997 South Korea has been participating in the financing of the ISTC. The government of the Republic of Korea appropriated $2.7 million for this, and a nongovernmental organization, the Korean Atomic Energy Research Institute, donated $1.1 million.[48]

CANADA. In June 2002, an agreement between the government of the Russian Federation and the government of Canada concerning the elimination of chemical weapons was signed. Canada allocated Can$5 million for construction of the infrastructure of the CW elimination facility in the town of Shchuch'ye. These funds will be directly transferred to the account of the Russian Munitions Agency, which is the executive agent for the Russian side under the agreement. This will allow the agency to conclude contracts with Russian contractors for work on facility infrastructure.

Results of Assistance to Russia

The results and the efficiency of the foreign assistance programs to Russia to eliminate the Cold War legacy are the subject of serious debate in Russia as well as abroad. Some Russian experts and politicians assert that the Western states "are luring us into a disarmament race," that "there's no such thing as a free lunch," and the like. But, more seriously, there is a reluctance to agree to assistance rendered only on certain nonnegotiable terms and conditions as well as a belief that the assistance being offered is insufficient to resolve the problem Russia faces. In the West, as in other parts of the world, the concern is that assistance to Russia has been much too little, and that the problems solved so far—for the amount of funds spent—pale in comparison with the magnitude to the problems that remain.

Since the beginning of the implementation of the CTR programs, Russia and the United States have succeeded in several areas. Assistance provided through the DOD allowed Russia, Ukraine, Kazakhstan, and Belarus to fulfill the START I conditions and eliminate strategic offensive arms. By May 2001, DOD had assisted in transporting to Russian storage facilities about 5,500 nuclear warheads removed

---

46. Ibid.

47. Tsutomu Arai and Nobumasa Akiyama, "Japan," in Einhorn and Flournoy, *Protecting against the Spread of Nuclear, Biological, and Chemical Weapons,* Volume 3: *International Responses.*

48. Yo-Up Lim, deputy director, Technology Cooperation Division 1, Ministry of Science and Technology, Republic of Korea, interview.

Table 1.13. Elimination in the NIS, including Russia, of Strategic Delivery Vehicles, as of May 2001

Vehicle	Number eliminated
Intercontinental ballistic missiles (ICBMs)	423
ICBM silos	383
Nuclear-powered ballistic-missile submarines	19
Submarine-launched ballistic missiles	209
Strategic bombers	85
Long-range air-launched cruise missiles	483

Source: Marsh et al., "Accomplishments of Selected Threat Reduction Programs," May 2001, www.ransac.org/new-web-site/fastfacts/programs_accomplish_rev4.html; and Wolfsthal et al., *Nuclear Status Report,* 3.

from strategic vehicle delivery systems in Russia, Ukraine, Kazakhstan, and Belarus (table 1.13) or kept by these states in storage facilities. Colonel-General Yevgeni Maslin, former head of the 12th Main Directorate of Russia's Ministry of Defense, noted:

> The Cooperative Threat Reduction Program has played an extremely positive role. Now it may be acknowledged that cooperation between Russia and the US, on the issues of safe and secure storage and transportation of nuclear warheads, has allowed us to start resolving the issues associated with prevention of the proliferation of nuclear weapons and has reduced the risk of nuclear terrorism. Therefore, Russia and the United States have equally resolved an issue regarding their national security. Thus, the matter at hand is the mutually beneficial program and the cooperative reduction of a common threat.[49]

In addition, U.S. assistance proved to be extremely important for the destruction of ballistic missiles, the elimination of ICBM silos, and the disposition of the strategic nuclear-fueled ballistic missile submarines (SSBN).

In particular, U.S. assistance played an important, if not decisive, role for Belarus, Ukraine, and especially Kazakhstan as they became de facto nonnuclear-weapon states through these efforts. Equipment and special vehicles received from the United States, France, and the UK aided Russia in ensuring the safe and secure storage and transport of nuclear weapons and provided a good start to solving a number of other acute problems.

To ensure the safe and secure storage of nuclear weapons, the United States supplied Russia with 123 sets of quick-fix equipment for the fast identification of tampering or security violations at nuclear weapons storage facilities; highly reliable protective fences, both with and without alarms; simulators; equipment

---

49. Yevgeni Maslin, "Cooperative Threat Reduction Program and the National Security Interests of Russia," in *Cooperative Threat Reduction Program: How Efficient?* ed. Ivan Safranchuk, Study Paper No. 13 (Moscow: PIR Center, January 2000), 6.

including lie detectors and drug and alcohol testing equipment to use with personnel at the facilities; computers and software for integrated weapons control; and an accounting system.

The issue of decommissioning SSBNs has been almost completely solved with the help of the United States. Today Russia's priority is to acquire foreign assistance for the comprehensive decommissioning of multipurpose nuclear submarines (SSN) as well as the reprocessing of spent nuclear fuel unloaded from the reactors of the SSBNs.

The results of DOE's activities to ensure the safety of weapons-grade nuclear materials in Russia are not as impressive but still very significant. By early 2002, complete protection systems were installed at facilities housing about 7 percent of such materials, and so-called rapid upgrades were implemented at facilities containing one-third of Russia's weapons-grade nuclear materials. It is expected that by the end of FY 2003 (that is, by September 2003) DOE will have provided complete protection for approximately one-fourth of the buildings and structures housing HEU and plutonium. The weapons materials storage facility at PO Mayak is close to completion. In spite of significant difficulties, the HEU-LEU deal is under way, bringing substantial export revenues to MINATOM.

Thus, ten years after the launch of CTR programs in 1992, international assistance has helped Russia solve a set of critical problems and carry out a share of the necessary work. These are the positive results of cooperation by Russia with other states to eliminate its Cold War legacy.

There have also been negative results from the decade of cooperation. By 2000, it had become clear that the scale of assistance necessary to solve the current problems had been grossly underestimated. Today the tough task is to estimate the amount of resources necessary for solving them in the coming decade.

In addition, serious problems have come to light that are impeding efficient cooperation between Russia and other countries. Differences in the concepts and positions of the United States and Russia led to a long-term suspension of U.S. assistance in the construction of the CW elimination facility. Donor states often express dissatisfaction with the fact that the Russian budget provides insufficient funds for the programs. Donors also are not ready to accept Russia's refusal to allow foreign inspectors access to all facilities receiving foreign assistance. In Russia, attempts by foreign monitors to verify how the external assistance is used are often met with suspicion. There is displeasure with the fact that the assistance does not fulfill all of Russia's needs. If these outstanding issues are not solved, there will be less hope for successful cooperation in the elimination of the Cold War legacy in this decade.

CHAPTER 2

Transport, Storage, and Elimination of Offensive Arms

The safe and secure transport and storage of nuclear warheads as well as the elimination of superfluous strategic offensive arms, including nuclear-fueled ballistic missile submarines (SSBNs) and silos for intercontinental ballistic missiles (ICBMs), are obvious priorities for international assistance programs targeted for Russia. Without international assistance, Russia is not capable of fulfilling its obligations under START I and cannot eliminate the strategic arms that are to be decommissioned in the first decade of the twenty-first century. Because Russia cannot solve the problem on its own, international strategic arms control arrangements could be undermined and the threat of ecological catastrophes and terrorist attacks could be prolonged.

International assistance to Russia is the most successful of all CTR programs. The Russian and the U.S. standpoints and approaches differ in a number of areas, however. The most essential difference is related to the U.S. reluctance to assist in the disposition of guided cruise missile submarines (SSGNs) and torpedo attack submarines (SSNs). The problem is that the United States assists Russia only in SSBNs although, according to unofficial Russian estimates, SSBNs comprise just 25 to 30 percent of the nuclear submarines slated for decommissioning. Russians also believe that it is necessary for the United States to provide financial assistance for the construction of residences for retiring officers who have completed their service in the rocket forces and at the sites of the 12th Main Directorate of the Russian Ministry of Defense (12th GUMO). These views are not supported by the United States.

Secure Transport and Storage of Nuclear Warheads

During the past decade, the United States, France, Great Britain, and Italy have provided assistance to Russia in the secure transport and storage of nuclear warheads. France provided Russia with 100 nuclear weapon transport containers, nuclear warhead dismantling equipment, and radiation monitoring instrumentation. A facility for the storage of nuclear weapons components was built with French assistance near Novosibirsk. Great Britain transferred to Russia 250 special containers and 20 armored vehicles for the transport of nuclear weapons. Other equipment was supplied by Italy. The United States, however, played the major part in assisting Russia in this area.

During this decade, such assistance has been provided only by the United States. DOD provides funding for the secure transport and storage of Russian nuclear war-

Table 2.1. U.S. Program Funding Status for the Safe Transport and Secure Storage of Nuclear Warheads, as of January 2001, millions of U.S. dollars

Programs	Notified	Obligated	Expended
Safety and security of nuclear weapons and related materials in the NIS	969.7	803.6	518.7
Safety and security of nuclear weapons and related materials in Russia	858.7	693.5	411.3
Secure transportation and storage	84.3	61.2	58.0
Safety and security of nuclear weapons storage sites	217.2	127.7	80.6

Source: Amy F. Woolf, *Nunn-Lugar Cooperative Threat Reduction Programs: Issues for Congress*, CRS Report for Congress, 97-1027-F (Washington, D.C.: Congressional Research Service, Library of Congress, March 23, 2001), CRS-7, CRS-29–30, www.ceip.org/files/projects/npp/pdf/ctrcongress.pdf. Data were calculated from tables in this report.

Note: Notified—administration officials must notify Congress at least 15 days in advance of its intent to obligate funds for a project (this can be done before an agreement is completed); obligated—after completing the agreement, the administration can set aside funds for a project; expended—this can take several years because funds are disbursed as work progresses.

heads. Funds are used for the purchase of vehicles and equipment necessary for nuclear weapons storage facilities in Russia. In the 1990s, the U.S. Congress allocated slightly more than $300 million. By January 1, 2001, just under $190 million ($61.2 million and $127.7 million) in contracts had been concluded and something less than $140 million ($58 million and 80.6 million) had been spent. The large gap between funds appropriated and funds disbursed is explained primarily by the inability of the United States and Russia to spend more than $100 million—out of the $217 million appropriated by the U.S. Congress—for securing the nuclear warhead storage facilities (table 2.1).

From FY 2000 to FY 2002, the United States decreased its assistance to Russia for the safe transport and secure storage of nuclear weapons. But for FY 2003, the George W. Bush administration requested that Congress increase funding for Russian nuclear weapons transportation security by approximately $10 million more than Congress had allocated in 2002 (table 2.2).

Transport of Nuclear Weapons

The transport of nuclear weapons is considered the weakest link in the system. Terrorist groups and criminals would find it easiest to get hold of nuclear weapons during transport. A transport accident—also an intentional "accident"—cannot be ruled out.

Table 2.2. U.S. Allocations to Russia for Safe Transport and Secure Storage of Nuclear Warheads, FY 2000–FY 2003, millions of U.S. dollars

Programs	2000	2001	2002	2003
Safe transport of nuclear weapons	15.2	14.0	9.5	19.7
Security of nuclear weapons storage sites	99.0	89.7	56.0	40.0

Sources: Hoehn, "Analysis of the Bush Administration's Fiscal Year 2003 Budget Requests";
 National Defense Authorization Act for FY 2000, Public Law 106-65, Section 1301;
 National Defense Authorization Act for FY 2001, Public Law 106-398, Section 1302;
 National Defense Authorization Act for FY 2002, Public Law 107-107, Section 1302.

From 1989 to 1993, the USSR (later, Russia) undertook massive shipments of strategic and tactical nuclear warheads in order to remove Soviet nuclear weapons from Central and Eastern Europe. Starting in 1990, it also removed them from regions of unrest and local conflict in the former Soviet Union. In 1991 it began to remove them from the NIS. The removals created the previously unknown threat of terrorist encroachment on the nuclear weapon stockpiles and, especially, on the warheads while en route. Independent Russian experts report that the shipments were completed by late 1993 and, on the whole, about 17,000 nuclear warheads were slated to be stored by the central arsenal of the 12th GUMO.[50]

During transport of nuclear warheads, accidents such as fire or explosion pose the greatest hazard. Special railcars and containers that can prevent warhead damage or unauthorized access by individuals, including criminals or terrorist groups, are necessary. The United States assisted Russia to ensure the safety of nuclear warhead shipments. U.S. assistance included:

■ Developing a continuous monitoring system to trace the warheads en route;

■ Funding the manufacture (in the Russian city of Tver but using equipment supplied by the United States) of 115 special railcars—including 15 cars equipped with satellite communications, instrumentational control over nuclear warheads, computer-based systems, and devices to maintain necessary temperature—as well as supplying two prototype cars;

■ Supplying 4,520 Kevlar blankets to protect nuclear warheads during transport;

■ Supplying 150 supercontainers to transport warheads; these supercontainers can withstand automatic gunfire and are equipped with protective features that make it impossible to tamper with them without special equipment (in 1997, 150 additional supercontainers were delivered to Russia by Great Britain); and

■ Supplying five mobile complexes (including cranes) designed to ameliorate the consequences of accidents during the transport of nuclear warheads.

Since 1993, the number of Russian shipments of nuclear warheads has decreased, but that does not eliminate the need to protect them from accidental

---

50. Litovkin, "Cooperation between the 12th Main Directorate."

damage or terrorist attack. Therefore continuous repair of the special vehicles and replacement of those that have exhausted their warranted service lives are necessary. In 1999, the U.S. DOD and the Russian Ministry of Defense signed a memorandum in which they agreed the United States would continue to assist with the maintenance and repair of the vehicles and for the partial replacement of the fleet.

Beginning in 2000, the areas of most U.S. aid to Russia for ensuring the safe transport of nuclear weapons have included:[51]

- Providing Russia's Ministry of Defense with transportation services to safely transport nuclear weapons from operational sites to central storage sites and dismantlement facilities;

- Enhancing the safety of 100 unheated nuclear weapons cargo railcars and 15 guard railcars;

- Assisting Russia's Ministry of Defense with the maintenance and certification of nuclear weapons railcars used to move nuclear weapons from operational sites to federal stockpile sites and dismantlement facilities; and

- Providing Russia's Ministry of Defense with equipment to enhance its ability to respond to a nuclear weapons transport accident, including data transfer and communications equipment and other specific equipment.

Storage Site Enhancement

Russian nuclear weapons storage facilities are usually located in thinly populated regions far from large cities. The storage facilities have several levels of protection and are designed to withstand high shock loads such as a direct gravity bomb hit. Russian experts believe that the real threat to the security of nuclear warheads in storage would be improper storage conditions or monitoring regimes, internal warhead defects, lack of scheduled maintenance, and criminal attempts by storage facility personnel who have access to the nuclear warheads.[52]

By and large, the security of Russian nuclear warheads does not currently raise the concern of specialists. After multiple visits to sites within the 12th GUMO where Russian strategic rocket forces (SRF) and navy nuclear weapons are stored as well as greater familiarization with the accounting and safeguard systems used by the Russian armed forces, U.S. Strategic Command senior officials were convinced that the loss or unauthorized use of a nuclear weapon was realistically impossible. Russian nuclear facilities are not less protected than U.S. facilities; in fact, some are even better safeguarded. One U.S. expert testified before Congress:

> General Eugene Habiger, the former Commander-in-Chief of the U.S. Strategic Command, visited nuclear weapons storage facilities in Russia to observe safety and security procedures on two occasions, in October 1997 and June 1998. He

---

51. U.S. Defense Threat Reduction Agency, Cooperative Threat Reduction, Russia Programs, www.dtra.mil/ctr/ctr_russia.html.

52. The most complete, detailed, and publicly available description of Russian warhead storage conditions and regime, their operating procedures, dismantling, and other important technical details is found in Litovkin, "Cooperation between the 12th Main Directorate," 13–17.

stated that he was impressed with what he saw, although he acknowledged the tour only focused on strategic nuclear weapons and provided no information about security procedures at storage facilities for nonstrategic nuclear weapons. He also noted that Russia lacked many high-tech devices the United States used to maintain security at its nuclear bases and seemed to rely more heavily on added manpower. But he stated that he did not have any serious concerns about the security of Russia's nuclear weapons.[53]

General Habiger was correct when he commented that at the Russian facilities housing nuclear weapons, safeguard reliability was achieved mainly by extra man-power instead of by state-of-the-art expensive electronic security systems. Labor costs little in Russia. At the same time, security systems installed on many nuclear weapon storage sites have exhausted their designed service lives; and the systems lack spare parts, instrumentation, and other hardware, and largely require replacement. The lack of funds and reductions in the size of the Russian armed forces points to the need for substantial external assistance to equip the nuclear weapon storage facilities with state-of-the-art security systems. The loyalty and reliability of the nuclear warhead–operating personnel is of great importance, including programs for the prevention of drug use.

Under the CTR programs, the United States has supplied Russia with equipment for 123 nuclear weapon storage facilities, including 25 facilities that hold SRF warheads.[54] By 2001, DOD had supplied to Russia:

- About 500 kilometers of power and alarm cable and about 200 kilometers of special perimeter fences;

- 59 computer systems, including 38 servers and the corresponding software;

- 80 sets of video surveillance equipment for facility protection;

- 10 snow plows, 50 mini-tractors, 11 maintenance cars, 16 power generators, and weather stations; and

- 10,000 drug analysis kits and 2 sets of polygraph equipment.

U.S. instructors trained the Russian officers how to operate this equipment. Also, in February 1998, the Security Assessment and Training Center was opened in the city of Sergiev Posad, near Moscow. The center will assist the Russian Ministry of Defense in creating a nuclear warhead accounting and monitoring system. The need for external help for nuclear weapon storage still remains.

---

53. Amy F. Woolf, "Nuclear Weapons in Russia: Safety, Security, and Control Issues," CRS Issue Brief for Congress, IB98038 (Washington, D.C.: Congressional Research Service, Library of Congress, April 12, 2002), CRS-5, www.fas.org/spp/starwars/crs/IB98038.pdf.

54. Jon B. Wolfsthal et al., eds., *Nuclear Status Report: Nuclear Weapons, Fissile Material, and Export Controls in the Former Soviet Union*, No. 6 (Washington, D.C.: Carnegie Endowment for International Peace, and Monterey, Calif.: Monterey Institute for International Studies, 2001), 37, http://cns.miis.edu/pubs/print/pdfs/nsr/status.pdf; U.S. Defense Threat Reduction Agency, "Cooperative Threat Reduction," www.dtra.mil/ctr/ctr_index.html.

Table 2.3. Soviet Strategic Arsenal in the Early 1990s

Weapons	Russia	Ukraine	Kazakhstan	Belarus	Total
ICBMs	1,037	176	104	81	1,398
SLBMs	940	0	0	0	940
Strategic bombers	82	40	40	0	162
SSBNs	62	0	0	0	62
Warheads	6,976	1,804	1,410	81	10,271

Source: *SIPRI Yearbook 1994* (Oxford: Oxford University Press, 1994), 179, 284–289, 294.

Note: As agreed under START I negotiations, including definitions.

Elimination of Strategic Weapons

By the early 1990s, the Soviet strategic offensive arsenal consisted of approximately 2,340 silos and mobile and naval launchers,[55] 62 SSBNs, and 162 strategic bombers (table 2.3). These delivery systems carried approximately 10,300 nuclear weapons (according to START I accounting rules). Approximately 80 percent of these strategic arms were deployed or stored in Russia. Other strategic arms were in Ukraine, Kazakhstan, and Belarus—all of which became independent states after the breakup of the Soviet Union. Kazakhstan and Belarus almost immediately decided to get rid of their nuclear weapons; Ukraine made the same decision only after some hesitation. From these decisions emerged the very complicated problem of dismantling and removing the strategic arms from these countries.

A reduction of Russian strategic arms was also under way, caused by changes in the external military threat to Russia. The main external threat—the West—had been altered. Moreover, Russia's economic collapse allowed it to maintain only a much smaller strategic arsenal than the USSR had.

Finally, between 1992 and 2001, it became necessary to dismantle, eliminate, or dispose of about 1,400 (ICBM and SLBM) launchers, 90 long-range bombers, 48 SSBNs, and more than 5,300 nuclear warheads (table 2.4).

The program for the elimination of surplus offensive strategic arms included:

- Elimination of ground-launched and sea-launched strategic missiles, as well as long-range bombers;

- Elimination of liquid-fuel and solid-fuel motors for missiles, to avoid environmental pollution;

- Elimination of ICBM silos and SLBM launchers;

- Rehabilitation of the land where deployment of Russian SRF units and formations were reduced; and

---

55. Note that the number of missiles always exceeds the number of launchers. Missiles are stored not only in launchers but also in storage and maintenance sites. In the strategic arms reduction treaties, only missiles that are associated with launchers are considered.

Table 2.4. Soviet/Russian Strategic Forces in 1990 and 2002

Weapons	1990 (USSR)		2002 (Russia)		Weapons decommissioned	
SSBNs	62		14[a]		48	
	Launchers	Warheads	Launchers	Warheads	Launchers	Warheads
ICBMs	1,398	6,612	706	3,011	692	3,601
SLBMs	940	2,804	232	1,072	708	1,732
Bombers	162	855[b]	72	868[b]	90	—[b]
Subtotal	2,500	10,271	1,010	4,951	1,490	5,320[c]

Sources: Wolfsthal et al., *Nuclear Status Report*, 3; *SIPRI Yearbook 2001: Armaments, Disarmament and International Security* (Oxford: Oxford University Press, 2001), 466; and Archive of Nuclear Data, "Table of USSR/Russian Strategic Offensive Force Loadings, 1981–2002" (New York: Natural Resources Defense Council, 2000), www.nrdc.org/nuclear/nudb/datab2.asp.

a. Operational. The total number of SSBNs accountable in START I is higher.

b. Accounting for the bomber's warheads is difficult. The 1990 number is the number determined using the START I accounting rules. The 2002 number is the actual number of warheads. The question is whether the number of deployed warheads was reduced in proportion to the reduction in the number of bombers.

c. This subtotal is approximate.

■ Safe transport of nuclear warheads removed from ballistic missiles to storage and dismantling sites; also safe transport of missile fuel to elimination sites.

By early 2001, the U.S. Congress expected to spend about $1.7 billion for DOD to implement a set of programs associated with the elimination of strategic arms inherited by the NIS (table 2.5). Less than two-thirds of that was actually spent. More than a half the funds allocated were intended for dismantling strategic weapons in Ukraine, Kazakhstan, and Belarus; for their partial in-situ elimination or transfer to Russia; and for other efforts to ensure that these states are, in fact, nonnuclear states. By the beginning of the twenty-first century, these tasks had been generally accomplished and the future costs (table 2.6) in Russia will mainly involve completing the construction of elimination facilities for ballistic missiles, their launchers, and—what is especially important—liquid-fuel and solid-fuel motors for missiles. The issue of how to cover the operational costs of these facilities with foreign funds is still debated.

It is also important to have an idea of the scale of the future reduction of Russian strategic forces in order to estimate resources necessary to dispose and eliminate Russian strategic arms that are to be retired during this decade. Although it is impossible to define precisely, it was announced officially that by the end of this decade Russia intends to have 1,500 strategic nuclear warheads.[56] The number of

---

56. Vladimir V. Putin, statement (in Russian), November 13, 2002, www.kremlin.ru.text/psmes/2000/11/11762.shtml.

Table 2.5. U.S. Funding for Programs to Dismantle Strategic Weapons, as of January 2001, millions of U.S. dollars

Location	Notified	Obligated	Expended
All NIS	1,697.0	1,397.0	1,048.0
Russia	729.9	598.6	396.6

Source: Amy F. Woolf, *Nunn-Lugar Cooperative Threat Reduction Programs: Issues for Congress,* CRS-7, CRS-29.

Table 2.6. U.S. Funding Status of Programs to Dismantle Strategic Weapons, FY 2000–FY 2003, millions of U.S. dollars

Location	2000	2001	2002	2003[a]
Russia	177.3	177.8	133.4	70.5
Ukraine	41.8	29.1	51.5	6.5

Source: Amy F. Woolf, *Nunn-Lugar Cooperative Threat Reduction Programs: Issues for Congress,* CRS-7, CRS-29.

a. Administration request.

strategic arms depends on the doctrine and plans for structuring the Russian armed forces (plans are revised from time to time), economic capabilities, arms production rates, retirement of arms from combat duty, timely repair and maintenance, the supply of spare parts, and the guaranteed service life and the possibilities for extending that service life. Limitations on the number of strategic arms, imposed by the international agreements and commitments, also play an important role.

Estimates in the West of future Russian strategic forces (see table 2.7) are based on open source information about guaranteed service lives of main weapons systems as well as the assumption that the ICBM Topol-M production rate will be 20–25 a year. The Topol-M production rate possibly needs refining because production of these missiles in recent years has decreased significantly. These data lead to the conclusion that by 2010, in addition to the arms already removed from combat duty, there will be an approximate reduction of more than 900 ballistic missiles, 7 SSBNs, about 60 long-range bombers, and 4,000–4,500 nuclear warheads. To accomplish this within the current decade, according to the Russian estimates done in 2000, 1,003 ICBMs and about 500 silos, 669 SLBMs, and 95 long-range bombers must be eliminated.[57]

Although U.S. views on future reductions of the Russian strategic arsenal are somewhat different, it can be assumed that reductions between 2001 and 2010 will be 2–2.5 times greater than during the 1990s. Therefore, when the supplying and installing of basic equipment is completed, the cost of running the facilities—

---

57. "Cooperative Threat Reduction," U.S. Department of Defense, www.defenselink.mil/pubs/ctr/.

Table 2.7. Russian Strategic Nuclear Forces in 2010, projected

Weapons	Delivery vehicles	Warheads
SS-27 Topol-M ICBM	230	230/690[a]
Delta IV-class SSBN with SS-N-23 SLBMs	7[b]/112[c]	448
Borei-class submarine[d]	2[b]/28[c]	168
Tu-95 intercontinental bomber	10	120
Tu-160 strategic bomber	10	120
Total	390	1,086–1,546

Sources: Wolfsthal et al., *Nuclear Status Report*, 5, 35; *SIPRI Yearbook 2001*, 466, 468.

a. The higher number will be the number of warheads if Russia withdraws from START II and decides to equip the Topol-M with three warheads.

b. Number of submarines.

c. Number of launchers installed on submarines.

d. Western experts believe that the first SSBN of the Borei class will have 12 SLBM launchers with 6 warheads on each SLBM; the second SSBN will have 12 SLBM launchers.

day-to-day operational costs, repair of equipment, requisitions of spare parts—will be significantly less. As of mid-2002, neither the United States nor any other donor state has agreed to allocate funds to pay for these operational costs.

In the past decade, U.S. assistance to eliminate Russian strategic arms has been mainly focused on supplies of equipment to dismantle missiles, mobile launchers, silos, and bombers; railcars for shipping missiles; and special tanker trucks to transport liquid missile fuel.

The difficulty of finding an environmentally benign method of disposing of liquid missile fuel and solid-fuel motors has played the greatest role in slowing down the ballistic missile elimination rate. There are 153,000 metric tons of liquid missile fuel and oxidizer and more than 900 solid-fuel motors weighing a total of 17,000 metric tons to be eliminated. The elimination of liquid missile fuel began at two sites near Krasnoyarsk in late 1999. The third facility of this type was to begin operation in 2001, near Nizhnyaya Salda.

Solid-fuel motors must be destroyed at bases near Perm and Votkinsk. The base near Perm has been built and tested, but it is being used at only one-third of its capability; an additional $10–$12 million will bring it up to full capacity. The base near Votkinsk will be used as a backup for the Perm base and will also become a site for the elimination of defective charges from SS-24 and SS-25 solid propellant missiles. Construction costs for Votinsk are estimated at $12.5 million. At present, the base is capable of eliminating 10 solid-fuel motors per year, but that needs to be increased to reach the scheduled rate of 60 per year.

To eliminate the SS-24 ICBM rail-based mobile launchers, there are plans to build an elimination facility near Bryansk in 2002. Its estimated cost is $6.7 million. At present, under the CTR program, $104,000 has been allocated to design the base.

The liquid-propellant ICBM elimination facility, commissioned in 1993 near Surovatikha, had been designed to disassemble missiles in accordance with the START I provisions. The additional elimination of strategic armaments, as well as changes in SS-18 ICBM elimination technology, require upgrading and increasing the facility's capacities to disassemble up to 50 ICBMs per year. Expert estimates show that an upgrade of the Surovatikha elimination facility would cost $20 million. The elimination of heavy bombers is carried out independently by Russian organizations using U.S. equipment.[58]

In the future, the highest costs—about $470 million in this decade—will be associated with the elimination of SSBNs. The nuclear submarine disposition program is being implemented slowly, however; only some of the nuclear submarines and 420 SLBM launchers have been decommissioned. In August 1998, the U.S. side committed to paying for work being done, including wages for personnel. Dismantling has been slowed because there is no place to put the fuel unloaded from the SSBNs. Problems remain regarding the storage and reprocessing of irradiated nuclear fuel (INF) and RW. The latter task has been partially resolved through the donation by the United States, Norway, and Japan of two floating LRW treatment facilities.

Russian specialists believe that it would be reasonable to manufacture the strategic arms elimination equipment in Russia, not import it from the United States. In addition, Russia has been dissatisfied by the refusal of the U.S. Congress to allocate money for the construction of housing for retired SRF officers. Seven out of the ten SRF complexes planned for reduction are located far from large cities and provide jobs not only for military personnel, including officers, but also for people living in adjacent towns and villages. As a result, tensions are rising at the prospect of mass unemployment as the rocket complexes are disbanded. Officers who have unique practical knowledge obtained through their work with nuclear weapons and missiles (for example, experts in the operation of energy installations, radio electronics, missile launching, maintenance facilities, and spacecraft) may find financial opportunities connected with WMD in the states of concern. To prevent mass unemployment in these locations, several thousand officers need to be relocated to places with well-developed industrial infrastructures. This would require about $100–$120 million for housing allowances.

Dismantling Nuclear Submarines

By June 2002, 21 SSBNs had been destroyed. By 2007, 41 more SSBNs should be gone. Under the Nunn-Lugar program, however, funds are allocated only for the scrapping of SSBNs and the elimination of SLBM launchers. The comprehensive decommissioning of nuclear submarines includes a myriad of other operations. In addition, issues associated with the disposition of other types of nuclear submarines have not yet been resolved.

By 2002, the Northern and Pacific Fleets had accumulated about 120 retired nuclear submarines (table 2.8); of these, more than 90 still contained nuclear fuel in

---

58. Wolfsthal et al., *Nuclear Status Report,* 48–50; U.S. Defense Threat Reduction Agency, "Cooperative Threat Reduction," www.dtra.mil/ctr/ctr_index.html.

Table 2.8. Decommissioned Submarines in Russia, 2002

	Northern Fleet	Pacific Fleet	Total
Decommissioned	116	75	191[a]
Stored with unloaded fuel	49	45	94

Sources: Boris Reznik, "The Militaries Hide Nuclear Waste Leak," *Izvestiya,* February 28, 2002; "Russia needs to dispose of nuclear subs," Associated Press, March 20, 2002; and Victor Akhunov, "Atomnye katastrofi pri utilizatsii isklucheny" (Nuclear catastrophes are impossible during the dismantlement process), *Izvestiya,* February 28, 2002.

a. Includes submarines decommissioned by the USSR between 1986 and 1991.

their reactors. Maintenance of one retired nuclear submarine costs about R4.5 million a year. In case of a serious accident, the contamination of an area of the Arctic Ocean or Pacific Ocean would severely undermine not only Russia's economic interests but also neighboring countries and do serious damage to the environment. Today, the Russian Federation is making significant efforts to implement the comprehensive dismantling of the nuclear submarines and their spent fuel, but the size of the effort greatly taxes the resources available to Russia.

THE SCALE OF THE PROBLEM OF SUBMARINE DISMANTLING. From 1958, when the USSR put into service its first nuclear submarine, until 2002, the Soviet Union/Russia has had the world's largest nuclear-powered fleet: about 260 submarine and surface ships.[59] There were 248 nuclear submarines of different types[60] built, including 91 SSBNs, as well as several nuclear cruisers, icebreakers, communications ships, and service ships. In addition to the SSBNs, the USSR/Russia built and still builds SSGNs and other types of nuclear submarines.

Until the mid-1980s, the nuclear submarine construction infrastructure did not include enterprises or entities capable of disposing of them safely and completely. Problems connected with the disposal of RW and INF were never resolved by the USSR. By the early 1990s, the nuclear submarines built in the 1960s and 1970s had exhausted their service lives, but neither the USSR nor Russia has had the technical or economic capabilities to scrap them. The economic crisis in Russia as well as the massive removal of SSBNs from combat duty have aggravated the situation.

According to mass media reports,[61] by the first half of 2002, Russia had totally decommissioned 191 nuclear submarines; approximately 70 of them were dismantled and nuclear fuel was unloaded from 97 of them. Approximately 120 nuclear

---

59. James Clay Moltz, "Russian Nuclear Submarine Dismantlement and the Naval Fuel Cycle," *Nonproliferation Review* 7, no.1 (Spring 2000): 77; James Clay Moltz and Tamara C. Robinson, "Dismantling Russia's Nuclear Subs: New Challenges to Nonproliferation," *Arms Control Today* 29, no. 4 (June 1999); and "The Russian Northern Fleet," Report No. 2 (Oslo: Bellona Foundation, 1996), www.bellona.no/en/international/russia/navy/northern_fleet/report_2-1996/index.html.

60. "The Arctic Nuclear Challenge," Report No. 3 (Oslo: Bellona Foundation, June 2001), www.bellona.no/en/international/russia/waste-mngmt/21133.html.

61. "The U.S. appropriated 500 million dollars for Russian nuclear sub dismantlement," Lenta.Ru (Rambler), May 27, 2002, www.lenta.ru.

Figure 2.1. Russian Nuclear Submarines Dismantled, cumulative, 1986–2002

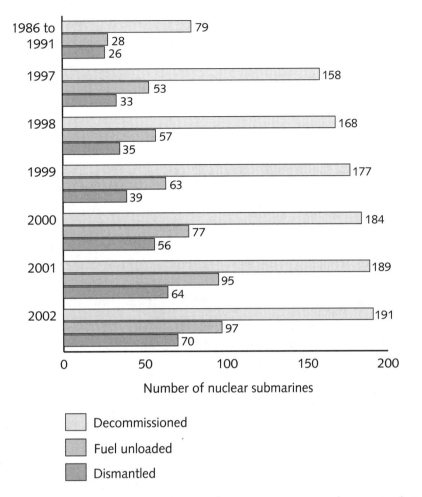

Number of nuclear submarines

☐ Decommissioned
▨ Fuel unloaded
▨ Dismantled

Source: "Decommissioned Subs Pose Risk of an Accident: Report," Associated Press, March 4, 2002.

submarines[62] and about 280 nuclear reactors are yet to be dismantled. The pace of nuclear submarine dismantlement is shown in figure 2.1, numbers are approximate because of the ongoing dismantlement/decommissioning process and because of a lack of information in the open press.[63]

62. "Decommissioned Subs Pose Risk of an Accident: Report," Associated Press, March 4, 2002.

63. V. A. Orlov, R. M. Timerbaev, A. V. Khlopkov, *Problemy iadernogo nerasprostraneniia v rossiisko-amerikanskikh otnosheniiakh: istoriia, vozmozhnosti i perspektivy dal'neishego vzaimodeistviia* (Nuclear nonproliferation in U.S.-Russia relations: Challenges and opportunities) (Moscow: PIR-TSentr polit. issledovanii: 2001), 178; P. L. Podvig, ed., *Strategicheskoe iadernoe vooruzhenie Rossii* (Russia's strategic nuclear arms) (Moscow: IzdAT, 1998), 229; "The U.S. appropriated 500 million dollars for Russian nuclear sub dismantlement," Lenta.Ru (Rambler), May 27, 2002, www.lenta.ru; *Bulletin of the Accounts Chamber of the Russian Federation* 42, no. 6 (2001); "Russia needs to dispose of nuclear subs," Associated Press, March 20, 2002; "Nuclear Submarine Dismantlement Issues," Press Service of the State Duma of the Russian Federation, March 19, 2002.

Western experts cite two reasons for the marginal conditions of the nuclear submarine disposition process in Russia.[64] First, before the "London Convention on the Prevention of Marine Pollution by Dumping of Wastes and Other Matter" was adopted in 1972, the Soviet Union (as well as other countries) had been dumping low-level LRW and other wastes, as well as the submarines themselves, in the sea—thereby avoiding costly and complex reprocessing and predisposal treatment. Because there had been no perceived need to build facilities for RW reprocessing, none were built.

Second, the Soviet Union's technology policy was oriented toward military production, and issues related to decommissioning of nuclear submarines that had finished their service lives were not treated as priorities and were not resolved. After construction at the shipyards and transfer to active naval duty, the nuclear submarines were used for training, then combat duty, and then, after their service lives ended, remained part of the navy's material assets. Until 1986, no official plans existed in the Soviet Union for dealing with nuclear submarines that had exhausted their service lives. Until the mid-1980s, all nuclear submarines (except for those that had suffered severe accidents), even if they had served for 25 years or more, continued to be repaired and returned to active duty in the navy.

THE DISMANTLING PROCESS. In 1986, the Soviet command established formal procedures for writing off and decommissioning nuclear submarines in several stages:[65]

- Withdrawing the ships from service (unloading weapons and other material, reducing the crew, relocating for mothballing);

- Unloading spent nuclear fuel prior to holding the fuel in special storage facilities for three years and eventual shipment to PO Mayak;

- Dismantling missile compartments (elimination of SLBM launchers);

- Decontaminating;

- Dismantling/cutting (separating the reactor compartment and cutting up "clean" compartments);

- Shipping reactor compartments to a long-term storage site; and

- Arranging for radiation monitoring.

These procedures are continuing. In July 1992, the government of the Russian Federation issued decree no. 514, "On the Measures Related to Pilot Operation of Submarines and Surface Ships Decommissioned from Active Navy Service," which was the basis for the test dismantling of nine submarines. The navy unloaded the fuel, and the submarines were taken to dismantling sites. The severed reactor compartments were returned to the navy, which was then responsible for ensuring their safe and secure storage. All reactor compartments were shipped to Saida Bay on the Kola Peninsula to be stored in floating cribs.

---

64. Moltz and Robinson, "Dismantling Russia's Nuclear Subs."
65. Podvig, ed., *Strategicheskoe iadernoe vooruzhenie Rossii*, 229.

According to the Russian government's decree no. 518, approved on May 28, 1998, MINATOM, not the Russian navy, was charged with the coordination of the nuclear submarine dismantlement process. Victor Akhunov, head of MINATOM's Department for the Environment and the Decommissioning of Nuclear Facilities, has said that by May 28, 1998, 121 nuclear submarines were waiting to be decommissioned; this included 111 nuclear submarines that were kept afloat after their nuclear fuel had been unloaded.[66] By late May 1998, some 30 submarines had defects in their ballast tanks and damage to their hulls and therefore required continuous attention to ensure they would remain watertight. With the increasing danger of radiation leakage, the situation at those bases was rather tense.

Since MINATOM took over the nuclear submarine decommissioning work in 1998, it has had two goals:

- Coordinating and funding the comprehensive decommissioning of nuclear submarines retired from the navy as well as nuclear technical support ships (for example, mother ships, special tankers, floating facilities for storage and transportation of waste); and

- Acquiring revenue through the sale of materials available after dismantling the nuclear submarines and surface ships; the proceeds of the investment of these funds will be used for future submarine disposition projects.

MINATOM began decommissioning nuclear submarines at the beginning of 1999. By that time, spent nuclear fuel was being removed from about four nuclear submarines per year. The following measures were taken to increase the fuel removal rate:

- Repairing existing navy mother ships;

- Reconditioning old mother ships; and

- Developing and implementing the plan to involve support ships of the Murmansk Shipping Company, which services the nuclear icebreakers.

In 2001, the construction of two on-shore nuclear submarine fuel-unloading facilities was completed: at the Zvezdochka plant site in the town of Severodvinsk and at the Zvezda plant site in the town of Bolshoi Kamen. Eight state-owned Russian enterprises are permitted to dismantle nuclear submarines:[67]

- Shipyard Nerpa;

- State Unitary Enterprise Zvezdochka;

- Shipyard Polyarninski;

- State Unitary Enterprise Sevmashpredpriyatie;

- Shipyard Tyazhminski;

- Shipyard Zvezda;

---

66. "Much has been done; more is going to be done," *Atom-Pressa*, No. 12, March 2002.
67. *Gazeta.Ru*, March 19, 2002.

- Russian Joint Stock Company Sevmorput;

- Shipyard Velyutinski.

At the present time, the disposition of each submarine is made according to a set procedure. MINATOM has a database on the current condition of each nuclear submarine and, on the basis of the database, the agency decides which submarines are to be scrapped first.

The pace of nuclear submarine dismantlement has grown substantially since MINATOM was charged with coordinating the process. Despite these improvements, Russia still does not have the infrastructure for full submarine dismantlement: Russia lacks the technical capacity for unloading nuclear fuel from the submarines; existing technical facilities are now basically focused on the unloading of SSBNs.

EXTRA-BUDGETARY FUNDS FOR DECOMMISSIONING NUCLEAR SUBMARINES. The major difficulty of decommissioning nuclear submarines is the lack of funding. In addition to funds budgeted specifically for decommissioning, Russia has three possible sources of additional funds for the project:

- External assistance from the United States, Norway, Great Britain, Japan, and other states;

- Sale of scrapped metal from nuclear submarines; and

- Sale of INF from nuclear submarines.

The commercial use of disposed nuclear submarine parts was permitted by Russian governmental decree no. 514. Shortly thereafter, however, it became clear that the commercial prospects of scrapping nuclear submarines were not as bright as had been believed. After the first nine nuclear submarines were scrapped, it turned out that the sale of metal from the scrapped submarines covered only 20 percent of the costs.[68]

As a preliminary proposal at a Nuclear Threat Initiative conference held on May 27, 2002, Senator Richard Lugar suggested the possibility of raising funds by selling INF.[69] The assumption was that nuclear fuel from a submarine, including fuel that has been irradiated, may be of a certain commercial value after reprocessing. The revenues received from reprocessing and sale could be a source of additional funding for disposing of nuclear submarines. According to preliminary estimates by Western experts, revenues from selling INF (or reprocessed INF) from one nuclear submarine could be $3–$4 million, a significant sum compared with the amount required for nuclear submarine disposition. But the experts are moderately skeptical about the prospects of INF sales. First, it is necessary to have accurate data on the isotopic composition of the INF intended for reprocessing and sale. Open

---

68. Valeri Lebedev, "We have to find an optimal solution to NS disposition," *Yaderny Kontrol* (in Russian) No. 6 (November–December 2000).

69. Richard Lugar, "Lugar envisions US-Russian front against terrorism and weapons proliferation" (speech at Nuclear Threat Initiative Conference, "Reducing the Threats from Weapons of Mass Destruction and Building a Global Coalition against Catastrophic Terrorism," Moscow, Russia, May 27, 2002), 3, www.nti.org/c_press/c_index.html.

sources contain only general information on this. Thus, according to information from the Nuclear Threat Initiative, the majority of Russian nuclear submarines (excluding 24 submarines that use uranium fuel enriched to about 90 percent) use uranium fuel enriched from 21 percent to 45 percent. Second, to use INF from nuclear submarines it is necessary to modify existing equipment, which requires additional investments. Third, a certain portion of INF in storage is damaged "due to the time factor" and requires more cautious and costly handling than normal fuel unloaded with the use of standard procedures.

Note that the United States assists Russia in disposing of the nuclear-fueled ballistic missile submarines; it does not fund the disposition of multipurpose nuclear submarines. Several other assistance programs help Russia dispose of multipurpose nuclear submarines.

AMEC PROGRAM. In March 1995 Jorgen Kosmo, the Norwegian minister of defense, proposed to the Russian defense minister and the U.S. secretary of defense that they should start working on reducing the damaging effects to the environment from military operations in the Arctic region. In 1996 after a series of consultations, the declaration on Arctic Military Environmental Cooperation (AMEC) was signed although it is not legally binding. The objective of the program is to reduce the impact on the environment in the Arctic region of military operations. Article 5 of the declaration states that all three parties must pay for participation in the AMEC program. It was not stated, however, that the cash contributions should be equal. By the end of 1997, the United States had invested in AMEC $1.8 million; Norway, $640 thousand; and Russia, $2 million. In 1998, the United States linked the CTR programs with AMEC to expedite the difficult and slow process of allocating funds under Nunn-Lugar programs. It was expected that allocating money through AMEC would speed up the resolution of problems associated with nuclear submarine INF and SSBN disposition.

Seven projects are financed under AMEC; five are related to nuclear submarine disposition:

- Development of a prototype container for nuclear submarine INF interim storage and transport;

- Development of technology for nuclear submarine LRW management;

- Review and application of nuclear submarine solid radioactive waste (SRW) compaction technologies;

- Review of technologies and procedures for nuclear submarine SRW interim storage; and

- Overall radiation monitoring.

After the decision was made to coordinate efforts of CTR programs and AMEC, the United States increased AMEC funding. Thus, in 1998, the U.S. Congress allocated $5 million, and in 1999 it allocated $4 million more. Norway and Russia were spending $1.6–$2 million annually.

In 1999, however, the U.S. Congress prohibited DOD from participating in AMEC projects where the use of Nunn-Lugar program funds had already been prohibited by Congress. In practice, this meant that U.S. participation in AMEC was reduced to projects directly related to SSBN disposition.[70] At present, the AMEC program is focused on the construction of needed infrastructure for INF and RW management on the Kola Peninsula and on the development of transport containers for nuclear submarine INF.

Japanese assistance programs to russia. On October 13, 1993, the "Agreement between the Government of Japan and the Government of the Russian Federation on Cooperation Concerning Assistance in Elimination of Nuclear Weapons Subject to Elimination in the Russian Federation and on Establishing of the Committee for Cooperation for these Purposes" was concluded.[71] Both Russia and Japan decided that a special Committee for Cooperation should be created to determine the best methods of cooperation, develop corresponding projects, receive financing to implement these projects, and control the cooperation.

In accordance with the 1993 agreement, Japan provided monetary assistance and specialized equipment for construction of the LRW treatment infrastructure.[72] By 1999, Japan had provided, in total, $70 million to the Committee for Cooperation.

In May 1999, after the Japanese minister of foreign affairs visited Russia, the two countries announced a new bilateral initiative for denuclearization, disarmament, and nonproliferation.[73] On the Japanese side, the most important initiative was the plan for disposition of decommissioned nuclear submarines in the Far East, which pursued the following projects:

■ Financing of unloading of INF from nuclear submarines and transporting it to storage locations;

■ Constructing an INF storage facility at the Zvezda shipyard;

■ Renovating selected railroads for INF transport;

■ Renovating the tanker Pinega for transportation of INF containers from nuclear submarines to railroad terminals; and

■ Disposing of decommissioned model no. 671 (Victor) multipurpose nuclear submarines at the Zvezda shipyard.

---

70. National Defense Authorization Act, 1999, Sec. 327; see also Steven G. Sawhill, "Cleaning up the Arctic's Cold War Legacy: Nuclear Waste and Arctic Military Environmental Cooperation," *Cooperation and Conflict* 35, no. 1 (March 2000): 223–236, www.umu.se/cerum/publikationer/pdfs/ NSB_1_00_6_5.pdf.

71. Database of official documents, Russian Federation, npa-gov.garweb.ru:8080/public/ default.asp?no=2440975.

72. Arai and Akiyama, "Japan," in Einhorn and Flournoy, *Protecting against the Spread of Nuclear, Biological, and Chemical Weapons,* Volume 3: *International Responses.*

73. Ministry of Foreign Affairs of Japan, "Japan-Russian Federation Joint Efforts for Disarmament and Environmental Protection," May 29, 1999, www.mofa.go.jp/region/europe/russia/ fmv9905/joint.html.

RESOURCES NEEDED FOR NUCLEAR SUBMARINE DISPOSITION IN RUSSIA.
To determine the cost of disposing of nuclear submarines, one needs to define what disposing means. The nuclear submarine disposition process can be divided into four major stages: decommissioning, unloading spent nuclear fuel, cutting out the reactor compartment and dismantling other compartments, and disposal of the reactor compartments. Complex disposition includes the creation and maintenance of a complete infrastructure for nuclear submarine disposition.

Nikolai Kalistratov, the director of the State Unitary Enterprise Zvezdochka,[74] stated that unloading spent nuclear fuel from one nuclear submarine costs $1.5 million, and the whole disposition process for one submarine requires $6 million. Other data show that the cutting of a defueled nuclear submarine in dry dock costs $4.25 million.[75] These numbers apply to an undamaged, fully operational SSBN. The dismantling problem is complicated by what Vladimir Klimov, chairman of the State Duma Subcommittee for the Use of Atomic Energy, says is the "time factor."[76]

Therefore, accounting for the upgrading of service ships that unload nuclear submarines and the elimination of SLBM launchers, the disposition cost of one SSBN may be as high as $15 million. Nuclear submarine disposition in Russia still costs less than in the United States, however, where the disposition of one nuclear submarine costs, by different estimates, between $20 and $40 million.

Although dismantling is cheaper in Russia, the amount of assistance provided by donor countries is inadequate for the challenges faced by Russia. To dispose of 15 nuclear submarines annually and create the infrastructure (now lacking) for each year between 2001 and 2005, it was necessary to augment Russia's budgeted funds (targeted at R1–R1.2 billion) for nuclear submarine disposition, with foreign financial contributions of $70–$80 million annually. Victor Akhunov, head of MINATOM's Department for the Environment and the Decommissioning of Nuclear Facilities, believes that the financial needs of the nuclear submarine disposition program are R2.5 billion per year, at March 2002 prices.[77] The total disposition of all currently decommissioned nuclear submarines—including the creation of necessary infrastructure, additional process and transportation capacities, and all required operations—will require $2–$3 billion.[78]

MINATOM believes that if these funds were available, the unloading of spent nuclear fuel from nuclear submarines would be completed by 2007, with the disposition completed by 2010. This assumes that at the beginning of 2002 Russia has about 100 unloaded nuclear submarines and the unloading rate is about 18–20 submarines per year.[79] All the submarines could then be unloaded by 2007. If foreign assistance is unavailable, the nuclear submarine disposition program completion date would need to be extended to 2020, an extremely negative devel-

---

74. Ibid.

75. Moltz, "Russian Nuclear Submarine Dismantlement," 79.

76. "Nuclear Submarines Dismantlement Issues," Press Service of the State Duma of the Russian Federation, March 19, 2002.

77. Ibid.

78. Valery Semin, "International Financial and Technical Assistance to Russia in Strengthening the Nonproliferation Regime," *Yaderny Kontrol* (in Russian) No. 5 (September–October 2001).

79. "Much has been done; more is going to be done," *Atom-Pressa*, No. 12, March 2002.

opment for environmental safety in the Russian Federation because of the current condition of its nuclear submarines.

MAJOR PROBLEMS OF DISMANTLING THE SUBMARINES. Currently there are four main technical problems associated with nuclear submarine disposition:[80]

- Storage and transport of spent nuclear fuel. After spent nuclear fuel has been unloaded from the reactor of a nuclear submarine, it must be stored for three years in the fleet's storage facilities and then shipped by special train to PO Mayak. Because of a lack of trains and storage at PO Mayak, the shipments are less frequent than they should be. Therefore, up to 80 percent of decommissioned nuclear submarines are still afloat with nuclear fuel unloaded. For the safe and secure storage and transport of the unloaded fuel, special metal-concrete containers have been manufactured and 48 containers of that type have been provided for the unloading of four submarines.

- Disposal of liquid and solid RW. During the dismantling of a submarine, large amounts of liquid and solid nuclear waste are accumulated and placed in storage facilities for long periods of time. Currently these facilities are obsolete and the waste is stored inappropriately. MINATOM recently attempted to solve the problem of nuclear waste disposal by putting two stationary, on-shore waste disposal facilities into operation at the Zvezda and Zvezdochka plants. Other refinements are needed, and work is in progress.

- Slow pace of operation at existing nuclear submarine dismantling facilities.

- Lack of specially furnished storage facilities. Such facilities are needed for reactor compartments with high levels of radioactivity. They need to be stored safely for long periods of time.

Exact data on the number of SSGNs and SSNs due for dismantling are difficult to find in the press. One estimate is that the total number of decommissioned SSGNs and SSNs is about 120 units.[81] Another estimate puts the number at about 150 units as of 2002.[82] On the basis of these assumptions and considering estimates of the cost to dismantle a single submarine, the fact that some of SSGNs and SSNs have already been dismantled, and that the dismantling of the SSBNs still will be financed by the United States, one can estimate that about $1 billion is needed for complete dismantlement of Russian SSGNs and SSNs.

---

80. Nikolai G. Mormul, *Katastrofy pod vodoi: gibel' podvodnykh lodok v epokhu kholodnoi voiny* (Underwater catastrophe) (Murmansk: Elteko, 1999), 512; Moltz and Robinson, "Dismantling Russia's Nuclear Subs."
81. "The Arctic Nuclear Challenge."
82. Podvig, ed., *Strategicheskoe iadernoe vooruzhenie Rossii*, 229.

CHAPTER 3

Security and Disposal of Nuclear Materials

After the demise of the USSR, the privileged yet simultaneously rigidly controlled nuclear complex that Russia inherited faced a number of unexplored problems. The situation posed a serious challenge to the international nonproliferation regime. For states of concern, the materials and the scientific and technological knowledge needed to build nuclear weapons are of great value. Russia possesses both, and in large amounts. Therefore, the prevention of threats that may be posed by the Russian nuclear complex is as important a task for the world community as for Russia itself. Considering Russia's economic difficulties, the United States and a number of other democratic states are pursuing two groups of programs targeted to reduce the threat of nuclear materials and sensitive-knowledge proliferation:

■ Physical protection of nuclear materials, their control and accounting; and

■ Reduction of stockpiles of nuclear materials and a halt to their production.

Materials Protection, Control, and Accounting

In the USSR, the secure storage of nuclear materials was ensured by stringent secret service controls, extensive constraints on freedoms (including the freedom of movement) of the nuclear industry employees who worked with nuclear materials, and the employees' own feelings of strict personal responsibility. After the collapse of USSR, state and police control weakened, including control in the closed administrative-territorial formations (CATF) within MINATOM, and the morale of nuclear enterprise employees has changed.[83] This has required the establishment of a new system for the physical protection of nuclear materials, control, and accounting (MPC&A), a system based on scientific foundations and state-of-the-art equipment and programs to reduce the effects of human fallibility. The difficult economic situation in Russia does not allow this task to be resolved with funding only from Russia. Ongoing improvement of the MPC&A system requires international assistance.

---

83. V. V. Erastov and N. N. Redin, "Current Situation with Improvement of Nuclear Materials Physical Protection, Control, and Accounting System in Minatom" (paper presented at the international nuclear materials physical protection, control, and accounting conference, Obninsk, Russia, March 9–14, 1997), vol. 1, p. 4.

Magnitude of the Problem

The highest threat, in terms of proliferation, is posed by HEU (more than 20 percent enrichment of uranium 235 content) and weapons-grade or weapons-usable plutonium. In Russia, there is no official publicly available information on these stockpiles. The available estimates are based on analyses of the plutonium production reactors' operational modes, enrichment capacities, nuclear weapons tests, the rate of dismantlement of nuclear weapons, the reduction of HEU amounts under the implementation of the U.S.-Russia HEU-LEU agreement, and other indirect factors. For example, the dismantling of nuclear weapons results in an increase in the amount of HEU, which requires enhanced safeguarding. At the same time, this amount is being reduced through the U.S.-Russia HEU-LEU agreement.

Experts estimate that the USSR/Russia has produced 120–150 tons of weapons-usable plutonium and 1,000–1,350 tons of HEU with more than 90 percent enrichment of uranium 235 content.[84] In the mid-1990s, it was assumed that about 30 percent of this material was still in warheads.[85] In early 2001, the U.S. government stated that Russia had 603 tons of HEU and weapons-usable plutonium[86]—very attractive to thieves—and that 252 buildings housing the nuclear materials safeguard systems of 40 Russian enterprises needed enhanced security.[87]

The stockpiles of weapons-grade nuclear material are scattered at several dozen enterprises over the whole of Russia. Although he did not clarify the weapons usability of the materials, Valentin Ivanov, the former first deputy minister of atomic energy, has stated that in Russia "nuclear materials are located at 61 organizations."[88] Most of the nuclear material is located in MINATOM's CATFs as well as in some enterprises and research institutes near Moscow. The amount of nuclear material in these facilities varies from several kilograms up to several dozen tons.

It is still a backbreaking task for Russia to provide these facilities and materials with the modern MPC&A systems. Funding planned for programs called the "State System for Control and Accounting of Nuclear Materials" and the "State System for Control and Accounting of Radioactive Substances and Waste," incorporated in the federal special program, "Nuclear and Radiation Safety of Russia for 2000–2006," and approved by governmental decree no. 149 on February 22, 2000, is about R70 million for seven years. This is approximately 30 times less than actually needed.[89] This amount does not include the costs of improving the nuclear materi-

---

84. Accounting of non-weapons-grade HEU (for example, fuel used by the navy) increases the estimates by several hundred tons. David Albright, an expert in this field, believes that by the end of 1999, Russia had 130 (±20 percent) tons of weapons-grade plutonium and 970 (±30 percent) tons of weapons-grade HEU. See "Summary Table: Production and Status of Military Stocks of Fissile Material, end of 1999," www.isis-online.org/.

85. David Albright, Frans Berkhout, and William Walker, *Plutonium and Highly Enriched Uranium 1996: World Inventories, Capabilities, and Policies* (New York: Oxford University Press, 1997).

86. This estimate evidently accounts for weapons-grade materials from nuclear weapons and may be covered by U.S.-Russia cooperation in the field of MPC&A system improvement.

87. "Nuclear Nonproliferation: Security of Russia's Nuclear Material Improving; Further Enhancements Needed," Report No. GAO-01-312, 1.

88. Press release no. 743, Press Center of the Government of the Russian Federation, September 28, 2000.

89. Ibid.

als control and accounting system but does include control and accounting system costs for radioactive materials, which pose significantly fewer hazards.

U.S.-Russia MPC&A Cooperation

At the present time, cooperation is implemented under the "Agreement between the Government of the United States of America and the Government of the Russian Federation Concerning Control, Accounting and Physical Protection of Nuclear Material," of October 2, 1999, signed by Yevgeni Adamov, the former minister of the Russian Federation for atomic energy, and Bill Richardson, the former U.S. secretary of energy. Its main objective is to reduce the threat that has resulted from the low level of safety and security for weapons-grade materials. Joint programs are being implemented to:

■ Improve MPC&A systems;

■ Consolidate and convert nuclear weapons materials;

■ Train personnel in MPC&A; and

■ Develop a legal foundation.

GOVERNMENT-TO-GOVERNMENT PROGRAMS AND COOPERATION WITH DOD. Since 1992, activities to improve MPC&A at Russian facilities have been financed with funds allocated by DOD for the CTR program. In turn, DOE has coordinated implementation of the relevant projects in the United States. In 1993, DOD and MINATOM signed an agreement on the development of a national system for the physical protection, control, and accounting of civilian nuclear materials.[90]

MPC&A projects, financed through the DOD, are integrated into the so-called government-to-government program.[91] From FY 1991 through FY 1995, the U.S. Congress allocated $63.5 million for MPC&A activities under the CTR program (table 3.1); $3.8 million was spent for this purpose and about 50 percent of the funds were allocated to Russia.[92]

The slow pace of the government-to-government program was due to:

■ Difficulties in getting agreement on access procedures for the U.S. monitors to facilities having direct-use materials. In 1994, the United States proposed a demonstration project at two facilities for the fabrication of nuclear fuel from HEU, but MINATOM rejected this proposal due to the possibility of access to

90. Office of International Affairs, National Research Council, *Proliferation Concerns: Assessing U.S. Efforts to Help Contain Nuclear and Other Dangerous Materials and Technologies in the Former Soviet Union* (Washington, D.C.: National Academies Press, 1997), www.nap.edu/books/0309057418/html/index.html.

91. This cooperation covered materials located in Kazakhstan, Ukraine, and Belarus in addition to Russia.

92. "Nuclear Nonproliferation: Status of U.S. Efforts to Improve Nuclear Material Controls in Newly Independent States," Report No. GAO/NSIAD/RCED-96-89 (Washington, D.C.: U.S. General Accounting Office, March 1996), 29, www.nti.org/db/nisprofs/russia/fulltext/gaorpts/gaompca.pdf.

Table 3.1. Funding for MPC&A under Government-to-Government Program, 1991–1995, millions of U.S. dollars

Country	Allocated	Contracts signed	Disbursed
Russia	30.0	27.5	2.0
Ukraine	22.5	21.5	0.7
Kazakhstan	8.0	7.6	1.1
Belarus	3.0	2.6	0
Total	63.5	59.2	3.8

Source: "Nuclear Nonproliferation: Status of U.S. Efforts to Improve Nuclear Material Controls in Newly Independent States," Report No. GAO/NSIAD/RCED-96-89 (Washington, D.C.: U.S. General Accounting Office, March 1996), www.nti.org/db/nisprofs/russia/fulltext/gaorpts/gaompca.pdf.

classified information. MINATOM insisted on a preliminary testing of the relevant procedures at a facility where low-enriched fuel was used. As a result, the United States agreed to finance only the activities carried out at the Mashinostroitelni Zavod (Machine-Building Plant) in the city of Electrostal (Moscow region).

- MINATOM's reluctance to acknowledge the regulatory role of Gosatomnadzor in Russia.[93] MINATOM took this position because of uncertainty concerning the status of Gosatomnadzor caused by omissions in relevant Russian legislation.

- U.S. legislative provisions stipulating that allocated funds for the CTR program needed to be spent in the United States (the "buy American" principle).[94] MINATOM complained that these funds could have been spent more efficiently in Russia for Russian equipment and wages for Russian specialists.

During the initial stage of cooperation, the Russian Methodological and Training Center (RMTC) on Nuclear Materials Control and Accounting was established at the Obninsk Institute for Physics and Power Engineering (IPPE) to train Russian specialists in modern techniques for the development, implementation, and operation of MPC&A systems. Only in 1995 did the government-to-government program start to cover facilities where direct-use nuclear material was stored and used. In June 1995, during the Gore-Chernomyrdin commission meeting, an agreement was signed to extend the program to the HEU fuel fabrication line at the Electrostal *Mashinostroitelni Zavod*, the Scientific Industrial Association (NPO) Luch in Podolsk (Moscow region), the Research Institute for Atomic Reactors (RIAR) in Dimitrovgrad (Ulyanovsk region), PO Mayak in Ozersk (Chelyabinsk region), and the IPPE in Obninsk (Kaluga region). In 1996, cooperation under the government-to-government program was expanded to 10 more MINATOM enterprises.[95] Starting in 1996, all programs in the area of MPC&A improvement have been financed by the U.S. DOE budget.

---

93. Ibid.
94. Wolfsthal et al., *Nuclear Status Report*.

Table 3.2. Funding for MPC&A under Laboratory-to-Laboratory Program, 1994–1995, millions of U.S. dollars

Fiscal year	Allocated	Contracts signed	Disbursed
1994	2.1	2.1	1.6
1995	15.0	15.0	12.7
Total	17.1	17.1	14.3

Source: "Nuclear Nonproliferation: Status of U.S. Efforts to Improve Nuclear Material Controls in Newly Independent States," Report No. GAO/NSIAD/RCED-96-89.

LABORATORY-TO-LABORATORY PROGRAM AND COOPERATION WITH DOE. In 1994, the DOE started a program eventually called the laboratory-to-laboratory program. It was based on the already existing business relations between U.S. national laboratories and Russian institutes and enterprises. This allowed them to avoid many problems inherent in the government-to-government program.[96] The most significant results of the MPC&A projects cooperatively implemented by the Russian enterprises and the U.S. national laboratories were the demonstration of a jointly designed system for nuclear materials control and accounting (C&A); agreements and contracts to improve the efficiency of the existing nuclear materials MPC&A systems and support of joint developments; contracts targeted to strengthen requirements for measurements done under the nuclear materials MPC&A improvement process; and contracts to design tamper indication devices. Russian participants in these cooperative efforts include the Russian Federal Nuclear Center (RFNC) All-Russian Research Institute of Experimental Physics (VNIIEF), RFNC All-Russian Research Institute of Technical Physics (VNIITF), Siberian Chemical Combine (SCC), the Bochvar Institute, VNII Avtomatiki, and others.

The much higher value of the laboratory-to-laboratory program compared with the government-to-government program is in part demonstrated by the monetary amounts spent on its implementation (table 3.2).

THE MPC&A PROGRAM. In February 1997, DOE merged the laboratory-to-laboratory and government-to-government programs into the MPC&A program. On the Russian side, DOE's partners were MINATOM, which controls the great majority of the Russian nuclear facilities, and Gosatomnadzor, which was coordinating U.S.-Russia cooperation at the nuclear facilities within the systems of the Ministry of Education, the Ministry of Economic Development and Trade, and others.[97] In addition, DOE concluded a cooperative agreement with the Russian navy, which had a number of independent nuclear facilities.

---

95. S. D. Lutsev, V. V. Erastov, and N. N. Redin, "Issues Related to the Coordination of International Cooperation between Minatom in the Field of Nuclear Materials Physical Protection, Control, and Accounting" (paper presented at the international nuclear materials physical protection, control, and accounting conference, Obninsk, Russia, March 9–14, 1997).

96. This program included the United States and Russia only; other former states of the USSR were not covered.

Table 3.3. Status of Installation of MPC&A Systems at Russian Facilities, 2001

Status	Buildings in civilian enterprise areas	Buildings in navy facility areas	Buildings in weapons laboratory areas	Total
Completed	51	21	9	81
Partially completed (rapid upgrades)	8	3	23	34
Work commenced	11	11	46	68
Work not commenced	19	1	49	69
Total	89	36	127	252

Source: "Nuclear Nonproliferation: Security of Russia's Nuclear Material Improving; Further Enhancements Needed," Report No. GAO-01-312 (Washington, D.C.: U.S. Government Accounting Office, February 28, 2001), 8, www.gao.gov/new.items/d01312.pdf.

By the start of 2001, under the MPC&A program, the U.S. Department of Energy had completed, fully or in part, the installation of nuclear materials security systems in 115 out of 252 buildings that housed 192 tons (32 percent) of weapons-grade nuclear materials that required special attention (table 3.3). Work was completely done in 81 buildings containing 86 tons (14 percent) of nuclear materials and rapid upgrades[98] were finished in 34 buildings containing 106 tons (18 percent) of nuclear materials. Work had also begun at facilities that contained an additional 130 tons of nuclear materials.[99]

While it has been noted that the buildings that have undergone rapid upgrades contain less weapons-grade nuclear material than those buildings that have not, note that cooperative efforts are being expanded into more and more sensitive facilities. At the same time, the large amount of nuclear materials (nearly 70 percent) contained in the buildings not covered by the upgrades speaks to the fact that the access problem still remains one of the main obstacles for cooperation.

97. Alexander Sanin, "Results of Nuclear Material and Nuclear Facilities' Physical Protection Systems Upgrades under the International Cooperation of Gosatomnadzor of Russia" (report presented at meeting of the PIR Center expert advisory council meeting, February 1, 2002).

98. "Rapid upgrades" refers to measures to eliminate elemental, but substantially important, deficiencies in the security of nuclear material and the creation of a baseline nuclear materials control system at a facility. Such measures may include walling up windows in buildings, reinforcement of walls, installation of reinforced locks and seals on nuclear material containers, arrangement for controlled access to areas where nuclear materials are stored and handled, and the introduction of the two-man rule (a procedure requiring the presence of at least two persons while nuclear materials are handled). An MPC&A system is considered complete when it includes several forms of automated surveillance systems (including motion detectors and video surveillance), a central alarm station, and a computer-based nuclear materials control and accounting system.

99. "Nuclear Nonproliferation: Security of Russia's Nuclear Material Improving; Further Enhancements Needed," Report No. GAO-01-312, 3.

Table 3.4. Funding for MPC&A Program, 1993–2003, millions of U.S. dollars

1993–1996	1997	1998	1999	2000	2001	2002	2003	Total
87.6	105.1	149.2	136.9	144.6	173.9	293	235	1325.3

Sources: For 1993–2000: Wolfsthal et al., *Nuclear Status Report;* for 2001: Howard Baker and Lloyd Cutler, *A Report Card on the Department of Energy's Nonproliferation Programs with Russia* (Washington, D.C.: Secretary of Energy Advisory Board, U.S. Department of Energy, January 10, 2001); for 2002 and 2003: "Anticipated FY 2003 DOE Nonproliferation Budget Requests and Comparison with FY 2002 Appropriations" (Washington, D.C.: RANSAC, January 4, 2002).

Notes: The substantial increase for 2002 depends on the U.S. Congress—in the post-September 11, 2001, atmosphere in the United States—allocating an additional $120 million. The estimate for 2003 reflects only the George W. Bush administration's request and does not take into account the possibility of additional financing, which may be approved later by Congress.

The four nuclear warhead assembling and dismantling facilities are significant in that they were not covered by the cooperative agreements. The probability that they will be included within the scope of U.S.-Russia cooperative programs is low, but in accordance with the restructuring program in the Russian nuclear weapons complex, it is planned that assembling and dismantling operations at two of the facilities will be discontinued by 2003.[100]

Expenditures for the MPC&A assistance program related to system improvements for Russia were $797.3 million in 1993–2001. Expenses incurred by the nuclear materials MPC&A program in the past and for the near future are shown in table 3.4.

SUSTAINABLE DEVELOPMENT AND OPERATION OF MPC&A SYSTEMS. By the late 1990s, a great amount of experience in upgrading the MPC&A systems at the Russian nuclear facilities had been accumulated. The installation of MPC&A systems was complete or rapid upgrades had been done at the majority of such facilities. Initially, it was planned that the U.S.-Russia nuclear materials MPC&A systems improvement program would be completed by 2002.[101] This did not occur because of a lack of financing as well as one more important factor: Experience gained during the operation of the implemented systems showed that installing state-of-the-art equipment is not sufficient to ensure the safety of nuclear materials.[102] In many instances the equipment supplied was improperly used because of economic difficulties, lack of operating experience with the modern equipment, and a low "safeguards culture" among personnel handling nuclear materials. Many

100. Lev Ryabev, first deputy minister of atomic energy (testimony to the State Duma, April 11, 2001, www.ransac.org/new-web-site/pub/nuclearnews/04.13.01.html.

101. "Nuclear Nonproliferation: Status of U.S. Efforts to Improve Nuclear Material Controls in Newly Independent States," Report No. GAO/NSIAD/RCED-96-89.

102. C. Gardner et al., "Sustainable Development of Physical Protection, Control and Accounting of Nuclear Materials: Political Review" (paper presented at the second international nuclear materials physical protection, control, and accounting conference, Obninsk, Russia, May 22–26, 2000).

staff are reluctant or unable to follow the necessary procedures, and they do not pay enough attention to nuclear materials safety.

DOE took account of this and started the Site Operations and Sustainability Program for the MPC&A in 1999. The program includes:[103]

- Warranty and equipment performance support, repair, and supply of spare parts;

- Training of personnel in the operation and maintenance of the new equipment; and

- Assistance in developing procedures and instructions on nuclear material control, accounting, and handling in accordance with the requirements of the new rules for control and accounting.

ASSISTANCE IN CREATING A NATIONAL INFRASTRUCTURE. Another important element of the MPC&A cooperation project is the creation of a national infrastructure. Its main components are:

- Regulatory and enforcement activities for nuclear material safety and security;

- Development of a federal information system for nuclear materials control and accounting; and

- MPC&A personnel training.

Cooperative efforts with DOE for the development of a regulatory foundation to ensure nuclear materials security has been undertaken by Gosatomnadzor, which acts as the regulatory authority, and by MINATOM, which is the executive body. DOE estimated that by early 2001, only about half the required regulations had been developed.[104] DOE also supports the regulatory and enforcement activities of Gosatomnadzor through the training of inspectors and the supplying of necessary inspection equipment.

DOE is assisting MINATOM in the development and implementation of the Federal Information System for Control and Accounting of Nuclear Materials (FIS-CANM). It is intended to reliably and in a timely way inform the executive bodies of the Russian Federation about the location, types, and amounts of nuclear materials and to detect possible thefts. At present, this system is connected to 15 nuclear industry enterprises.[105]

DOE also supports a number of MPC&A educational programs: RMTC and the Interbranch Special Training Center for physical protection issues, both located in Obninsk; and the two-year MPC&A intern training program at the Moscow Engineering Physics Institute (MEPhI).

CONSOLIDATION AND CONVERSION OF NUCLEAR MATERIALS. In Russia, weapons-grade nuclear material is located in hundreds of buildings on the property

---

103. "Nuclear Nonproliferation: Status of U.S. Efforts to Improve Nuclear Material Controls in Newly Independent States," Report No. GAO/NSIAD/RCED-96-89.

104. Ibid.

105. S. A. Sergeev, head of Nuclear Materials Control and Accounting Center of TsNIIAtominform (comment at meeting at the PIR Center, February 27, 2002).

of dozens of enterprises. The reduction of the number of nuclear weapons-grade material storage and handling facilities—as well as the conversion of the material to a form less attractive to a possible thief—may make achieving all the MPC&A program goals easier. Therefore, in 1999 DOE started the Material Conversion and Consolidation Program.

Plans under this program call for a reduction in the number of buildings and facilities containing nuclear weapons materials—it is planned that by 2010 nuclear weapons materials will be removed from 50 buildings located at 5 enterprises—and the conversion of 24 tons of HEU into LEU, which then cannot be used for nuclear weapons. If successful, the program would significantly decrease expenses associated with the installation and/or operation of MPC&A systems.

The Materials Conversion and Consolidation Program does not work, however. MINATOM is reluctant to identify specific facilities from which this material is to be withdrawn before a stand-alone agreement is concluded regarding this program. In addition, the nuclear industry enterprise management is reluctant to part with its nuclear materials, which are sometimes viewed as insurance for further funding under the MPC&A programs. At the same time, DOE has succeeded in reducing the number of buildings at enterprises where nuclear materials are stored that are not included in the conversion and consolidation program—at, for example, the IPPE in Obninsk,[106] the RIAR in Dimitrovgrad, and NPO Luch in Podolsk.[107]

FISSILE MATERIAL STORAGE FACILITY AT PO MAYAK. Under the CTR program financed through DOD, the United States is assisting Russia in the construction of a fissile material storage facility (FMSF) at PO Mayak in the city of Ozersk. The FMSF is designed to be used for the safe and secure storage of HEU and weapons-grade plutonium resulting from the dismantlement of Russian nuclear weapons.

The agreement between the DOD and MINATOM concerning the construction of the FMSF was concluded on October 5, 1992. Initially, there was a plan to build the storage facility in the city of Seversk, with the United States and Russia sharing the cost equally. But in 1994 the decision was made to locate the storage facility at the PO Mayak site. In April 1998, after a number of delays in implementing the project, Russia stated that it was impossible for it to participate in the FMSF construction funding at any substantial level. At present, it is planned that the first phase of the FMSF, capable of housing 25,000 containers of nuclear material, is to be completed by October 2002 at a cost of $413 million. The U.S. administration has also expressed its readiness to participate in the second phase of the storage facility, which will increase the facility's capacity by another 25,000 containers, pro-

106. A. P. Gorbachev et al., "Main Results of Cooperation between SSC RF IPPE and U.S. National Laboratories in the Field of Nuclear Material Physical Protection, Control, and Accounting: Improvement of Related Problems and MPC&A Development Prospects in SSC RF IPPE" (paper presented at the second international nuclear materials physical protection, control, and accounting conference, Obninsk, Russia, May 22–26, 2000).

107. V. V. Fomenko et al., "Portal Monitors in GosNII NPO Luch as a Subsystem of Integrated MPC&A System" (paper presented at the second international nuclear materials physical protection, control, and accounting conference, Obninsk, Russia, May 22–26, 2000).

vided that the necessary transparency measures are followed. The construction cost of the second phase is estimated to be $229 million.[108]

The U.S. Congress has set the conditions for funding construction of the FMSF. The United States and Russia must agree that the United States be able to confirm that:

- Nuclear materials are stored safely and securely;

- Stored nuclear materials are not used for military programs (the condition of irreversibility in the disposition of already stored nuclear materials); and

- Material to be stored in the FMSF must come only from dismantled nuclear weapons.

Agreement on the first two conditions was quick, but the confirmation that material in storage originated in a weapon created serious problems in negotiations. Initially it was assumed that the FMSF would receive easily identifiable HEU pits.[109] MINATOM, however, decided that the material would be modified prior to its placement in the FMSF. MINATOM wanted to conceal the composition of the nuclear weapons-grade material from International Atomic Energy Agency (IAEA) inspectors, who would eventually be involved in the verification of the security and irreversibility of this material. It was also forbidden for United States to have control of the material before reprocessing at PO Mayak.

DOE ASSESSMENT OF FUTURE COSTS OF THE MPC&A PROGRAM. DOE estimates the total expenditure for the program, through 2010, to be $2.2 billion.[110] This amount includes $823.1 million targeted for the completion of the equipment assembly by 2011, $711.8 million for maintaining the operation of MPC&A systems up to 2020, $241.3 million for program management, and $387.2 million for the consolidation and conversion of nuclear materials.[111] These estimates, however, do not consider the effects of the consolidation and conversion program on other cooperative programs.

Cooperation with the European Union

Russian cooperation with the European states in the area of safety and security for nuclear materials is not as comprehensive and wide-ranging as U.S.-Russia cooperation.

A characteristic example is the cooperation with the Euratom Safeguards Agency. Russian cooperation with this agency started in 1993 with the goal of establishing in Russia a state system for the control and accounting of nuclear materials in accordance with modern requirements.[112] The projects jointly implemented with this agency were not linked to the improvement of nuclear materials C&A systems

---

108. Wolfsthal et al., *Nuclear Status Report.*

109. The core of the warhead is made from fissile material.

110. This estimate was made in 2000 and therefore does not take into account changes that may have resulted from the review initiated by the September 11, 2001, events in the United States.

111. "Nuclear Nonproliferation: Status of U.S. Efforts to Improve Nuclear Material Controls in Newly Independent States," Report No. GAO/NSIAD/RCED-96-89.

Table 3.5. Financing of Cooperative Programs with Euratom Safeguards Agency, 1993–1999, millions of euros

1993	1994	1995	1996	1997	1998	1999	2000
0.5	1.0	1.8	3.0	0	2.0	1.4	1.3

Source: H. Kschwendt et al., "Past and Future Cooperation of the Euratom Safeguards Agency and the Russian Federation" (paper presented at the second international nuclear materials physical protection, control, and accounting conference, Obninsk, Russia, May 22–26, 2000).

at specific facilities. More important was the development of infrastructure: implementation of information systems, a regulatory foundation, development of inventory-taking methodologies, and personnel training, for example. From 1993 to 2000, this cooperation cost approximately €11 million; intermittent funding in the mid-1990s was caused by reorganization of the Europe/Russian cooperative program by the internal European Community (table 3.5).

The focus on specific projects and the small amounts allocated does not resolve the global task of reducing the threat of proliferation, but it does help to avoid the problems characteristic in U.S.-Russia cooperation. One of the main explanations is the sound working contacts established between both sides.

Among the main areas of cooperation between Russia and the European Union are upgrading the nuclear materials physical protection system; establishment of laboratories for analysis, identification of nuclear materials of unknown origin, and for nuclear metrology; training specialists in nuclear materials C&A; general scientific and technical support; technical support of nuclear materials C&A systems at specific facilities; modernizing instrumentation for nuclear materials safety, security, and C&A; modernizing methodological and metrological support of nuclear materials measurements; and modernizing the nuclear materials C&A system. Russian participants include the Bochvar Institute, MINATOM, Gosatomnadzor, and PO Mayak. European participants include the European Commission; Federal Ministry for Environmental Protection and Nuclear Reactor Safety (BMU, Germany); German Society for Reactor Safety; Transuraium Institute, Karlsrue, Germany; Reference Samples Institute, Gel, Belgium, and others.

Problems Implementing MPC&A Programs

A number of Russian specialists believe that the problems of implementing the cooperative programs with foreign states are due, in part, to unsatisfactory coordination of joint efforts, poor management of the U.S. programs, and the low safety culture and weak infrastructure in Russia.[113]

112. H. Kschwendt et al., "Past and Future Cooperation of the Euratom Safeguards Agency and the Russian Federation" (paper presented at the second international nuclear materials physical protection, control, and accounting conference, Obninsk, Russia, May 22–26, 2000).

113. This section generalizes data obtained through an analysis of open information sources, interviews with participants in the cooperative programs, and the roundtable discussion at the PIR Center on February 27, 2002.

UNSATISFACTORY COORDINATION OF JOINT EFFORTS. There has been a lack of coordination and consideration of possible cross-impact by programs implemented with U.S. assistance; and the MPC&A system improvement and programs for conversion/consolidation/disposition of nuclear weapon materials serve as examples of this. Also, sometimes Russian and U.S. partners interact poorly. The U.S. side often reserves the right to make the final decision on programs without considering opinions of the Russian representatives participating in the implementation of the joint programs.

POOR PROGRAM MANAGEMENT ON THE U.S. SIDE. Frequent substitution of the personnel involved in the implementation of joint projects affects cooperation among personnel as well as degrades the level of responsibility by individuals in charge of a specific project. In addition, many Russian participants point to the frequent changes of U.S. personnel as the main obstacle in resolving the access issue because changes of personnel prevent establishing good working relations and trust between the partners. Working groups at Russian facilities remain unchanged for several years, but the composition of the U.S. groups may change several times a year.

The lack of clear-cut criteria for assessing the efficiency of joint programs does not allow for the timely assessment of the cooperative results, does not reveal problems in implementation, or permit introduction of corrective measures.

A disregard for environmental conditions where the MPC&A systems are installed led to the assumption that the model MPC&A system would function as well in Russia as in, for example, the United States. This was proved false and resulted in a significant reevaluation of schedules and costs under the cooperative program.

The need for annual approval of the budget allocated for the cooperative program does not allow for long-term planning of joint projects.

The distribution of funds during the course of program implementation shows a bias toward spending a major portion of the allotted funds in the United States. The most optimistic assessments made by Russian specialists show that the nuclear facilities receive 30–40 percent. The majority of funds are spent in the United States to cover program management costs, costs of supervision, and other managerial expenses although funds might well be spent more efficiently in Russia.

LOW NUCLEAR SAFETY CULTURE. The poor state of knowledge about the nuclear weapons nonproliferation regime on the part of enterprise employees involved in the nuclear materials safeguards activities in Russia results in a lack of commitment to program goals. This reduces staff motivation to actively support the work being done in the area of nuclear materials physical protection and control.

Russian workers lack experience in operating state-of-the-art MPC&A technologies. The abrupt transition from accountant-like techniques of control and accounting used in the USSR to the use of high-tech equipment has brought into question the possibility of sustainable operation and performance of the systems.

Managers of the Russian nuclear industry enterprises put low priority on the installation of the MPC&A systems, expressed through their reluctance to spend the enterprise's funds for MPC&A system improvements. Strong doubts persist about the sustainability of the systems after U.S. financing ends. Another consequence of the low priority of the issue is that a significant number of employees involved in MPC&A activities split their responsibilities between MPC&A and other activities; often working on MPC&A is not their key work objective.

LOW LEVEL OF INFRASTRUCTURE DEVELOPMENT. Costs (financial, time, and human) of nonmaterial components—operations and training—at present already exceed the costs of equipment installation. Not having a feel for the results of investments in this area (an assistance efficiency assessment issue) reduces Russian motivation to spend as much as the U.S. side would like.

A weak regulatory structure in Russia has led to the unavailability of enterprise-specific control and accounting procedures and uncertainty about the amnesty issue.[114] This slows down the already slow pace of implementing modern MPC&A systems.

There is also a compatibility issue between the FISCANM and the information systems at different enterprises.

International Assistance for Ceasing Production and Disposing of Nuclear Weapons Materials

At present, Russia does not produce nuclear materials for weapons use. HEU production was stopped in 1988.[115] By September 1992, 10 out of 13 reactors used in the USSR/Russia to produce plutonium for weapons had been shut down. The three remaining reactors[116] continue to operate but are used only to supply electricity and heat. They produce 1–1.5 tons of plutonium per year,[117] which is not separated from the irradiated fuel.

International assistance for disposing of nuclear materials and terminating production includes:

■ Cooperation in the disposition of weapons-grade plutonium;

■ U.S.-Russia HEU-LEU conversion program; and

■ U.S.-Russia cooperation concerning the conversion of plutonium production reactors.

---

114. Enterprise management is afraid of being punished for possible discrepancies in accounting data; this did occur in the past. Also the initial physical inventory becomes an issue when shifting to the new MPC&A system.

115. Albright et al., *Plutonium and Highly Enriched Uranium 1996.*

116. Two are at the Siberian Chemical Combine (SCC) in Seversk (formerly called Tomsk-7) and one is at the Mining and Chemical Combine (MCC) in Zheleznogorsk (formerly called Krasnoyarsk-26).

117. Frank von Hippel (presentation at the International Nonproliferation Conference, Moscow, Russia, October 6–7, 2000).

Disposition of Weapons-Grade Plutonium

COOPERATION BETWEEN RUSSIA AND FRANCE. The agreement between the government of the Russian Federation and the government of France, "Concerning Cooperation in the Field of Civil Uses of Nuclear Materials Released as a Result of Elimination of Nuclear Weapons," was signed on November 12, 1992, and came into force on March 30, 1993. In accordance with this agreement, Russia and France implemented a four-year joint research program (AIDA-MOX) to study the possibility of using uranium and plutonium originally from weapons. The largest part of the research dealt with "the use of military plutonium and the corresponding fuel cycle of MOX fuel fabricated with military plutonium and its irradiation in the fast neutron reactors (BN-350, BN-600 and BN-800) and in thermal reactors (VVER-1000)." The goal of the joint research program was an assessment that would support "a decision on the use of plutonium (as MOX fuel) on an industrial scale in the Russian Federation." The program focused on six topics:

- Strategic approaches. Compile a list and assess possible strategies allowing for the disposition of nuclear materials of military origin;

- Reactor calculations. Calculate the possibility of converting VVER and BN reactors, which use uranium oxide fuel, to MOX fuel;

- Plutonium chemistry. Exchange information on techniques for the conversion of metal plutonium or its alloy into plutonium oxide, establish cooperation in the area of chemical conversion techniques, and identify corresponding pilot facilities;

- Fabrication of MOX fuel. Exchange information on techniques, concepts, and design of a MOX-fuel fabrication plant for BN reactors and thermal reactors; establish Russian-French cooperation in this area;

- Reprocessing of mixed fuel. Exchange data on techniques in use and the results obtained regarding the reprocessing of irradiated MOX fuel; and

- Efficient reactors. Identify of the best types of nuclear reactors for civilian power generation that would use military nuclear materials, considering environment, safety, economy, and nonproliferation.

Russia and France also agreed that each side, "in principle, bears the costs associated with activities and research it conducts in accordance with program." However, upon the decision of the coordinating committee, one of the sides may finance some of the other side's activities or compensate it for the relevant expenses.

The joint research resulted in a final report, which drew the following conclusions:[118]

- MOX fuel (up to 30 percent of the reactor core charge) can be used in certain VVER-1000 reactors after some reactor modifications similar to those done to

---

118. Yevgeni Kudryavtsev, "International Projects for Disposition of Weapons Plutonium: Results and Prospects," *Yaderny Kontrol* (in Russian) Nos. 34–35 (October–November 1997).

PWR-900 reactors in France. This approach may allow for the use of 270 kg of weapons-grade plutonium per VVER-1000 reactor per year;

■ MOX fuel (100 percent of the reactor core charge) can be used in a BN-600 reactor without a blanket of unenriched uranium. This is the most advanced option. It may be implemented within a reasonable time frame although some additional safety studies are necessary. In the short term, the conversion of a BN-600 reactor to having a hybrid (partial MOX-fuel core charge) core would allow the use of up to 240 kg of weapons-grade plutonium per reactor per year;

■ The baseline technology needed to convert weapons plutonium into MOX fuel to be used in the future Russian facility has been identified;

■ The capacity of the future Russian MOX-fuel fabrication facility is dependent on the fuel consumption capabilities of the existing Russian VVER-1000 and BN-600 reactors;

■ The BN-600 reactor, with a hybrid core, can consume up to 240 kg of weapons-grade plutonium a year; and

■ The four most advanced VVER-1000 reactors, at the Balakovo nuclear power plant, can consume a total of 1,080 kg per year (each at an annual consumption rate of 270 kg of weapons-grade plutonium).

The conclusion was that the total production capacity of the facility must be approximately 1,300 kg of weapons-grade plutonium a year, or about 30 tons of MOX fuel per year. On the Russian side, the IPPE at Obninsk; the Kurchatov Institute, a Russian research center; the RIAR (Dimitrovgrad); the Research Institute for Inorganic Materials (Moscow); and the Radium Institute (St. Petersburg) participated in the AIDA-MOX program. On the French side, the military division of the Commissariat à l'Energie Atomique and the companies Cogema, Framatom, and CGN participated.[119]

COOPERATION BETWEEN RUSSIA AND GERMANY. Cooperation between Russia and Germany concerning the disposition of surplus weapons-grade plutonium is based on an intergovernmental agreement regarding assistance to Russia to eliminate and reduce its nuclear and chemical weapons. The agreement was signed on December 16, 1992, and entered into force on March 7, 1993.[120] In particular, Germany committed itself to provide free assistance in the elimination of nuclear and chemical weapons on the territory of the Russian Federation in accordance with Russian obligations regarding arms limitation and disarmament.

In the framework of this agreement, a conceptual design for a pilot MOX-fuel fabrication facility to reprocess one metric ton of weapons-grade plutonium per year was accomplished. The Federal Special Design Institute of MINATOM (GSPI), PO Mayak, the Bochvar Institute, and Siemens participated in the work. It was planned that equipment from Germany (from a Siemens-owned Hanau plant) and

---

119. Vladimir Rybachenkov, "On International Cooperation of Russia in the Field of Disposition of Surplus Weapons Plutonium," *Yaderny Kontrol* (in Russian) No. 6 (November-December 2000).

120. Either side may terminate this agreement at any time by written notification.

Russia (from Complex 300 at PO Mayak) would be used. It was calculated that having small amounts of the MOX fuel fabricated by such a facility would cost 30 percent more than uranium fuel without even taking into account the cost of the metal plutonium, in part, because of the reprocessing costs. The fuel cost, however, may significantly decrease if production capacities increase. The construction cost for a stand-alone pilot facility at PO Mayak was estimated to be DM190 million. Calculations for the annual operating costs included all applicable Russian taxes.[121] Also, the possibility of using MOX fuel in the BN-600/BN-800 fast neutron reactors and the VVER-1000 reactors was confirmed.

COOPERATION AMONG RUSSIA, FRANCE, AND GERMANY. In 1998, Russia, Germany, and France decided to merge their efforts under a trilateral cooperative agreement, the AIDA-MOX 2 program, which was signed on June 2, 1998, in Moscow.[122] In 2000, Italy and Belgium joined the trilateral agreement.

In accordance with the 1998 agreement, design documentation and proposals for the construction schedule of the metal plutonium conversion facility (the CHEMOX Project) and the MOX-fuel fabrication facility (the DEMOX Project) capable of reprocessing 2.3 metric tons of weapons-grade plutonium per year is to be concluded. Within the same time period, preparations have been made for specifying design changes needed by the Russian reactors to use MOX fuel as well as final estimates prepared for the capital and operating costs. Preliminary estimates put the costs at about $1.7 billion.

It was planned that the MOX-fuel fabrication plant would be furnished with equipment transferred to Russia from a plant in Hanau that was mothballed in 1995. French officials stated that the plant commissioning was scheduled for 2007–2008, depending on the supply of the German equipment. Siemens, the owner of the Hanau plant, stated that although the United States and France had allocated DM500 million to support the project, the total cost of work would be about DM2 billion. Financing uncertainties and a lack of political support led Siemens to announce its refusal to begin dismantling the equipment and exporting it to Russia.[123]

COOPERATION BETWEEN RUSSIA AND CANADA. In November 1994, Russian-Canadian consultations were held in Moscow to consider the issue of using surplus Russian weapons-grade plutonium to fabricate MOX fuel for Canadian nuclear power plants with Canadian deuterium-uranium (CANDU) reactors,[124] and a memorandum of intent was signed. MINATOM expressed its interest in further study of the issue, and the Canadian side agreed to consider conducting a feasibility

121. Kudryavtsev, "International Projects for Disposition of Weapons Plutonium: Results and Prospects."

122. Embassy of France in Russia, official Web site, www.ambafrance.ru/rus/rus-france/aida2.asp.

123. Siemens Power Generation ultimately discarded plans to export the MOX-fuel fabrication equipment from the Hanau plant by stating its intention to start dismantling the enterprise. *Nuclear.Ru,* November 8, 2001.

124. Rybachenkov, "On International Cooperation of Russia in the Field of Disposition of Surplus Weapons Plutonium."

study regarding Russian construction of a MOX-fuel assembly fabrication complex with the intention of supplying the finished assemblies to Canada.

Work in this area was started in 1996, after an agreement between MINATOM and Canadian Atomic Energy of Canada, Ltd. (AECL) had been signed concerning the feasibility study, "Production of Uranium-Plutonium Fuel for CANDU Reactors with the Use of Weapons-Grade Plutonium." This resulted in the demonstration of a technical feasibility, in principle, of Russian fabrication of MOX fuel for use in CANDU reactors and then transporting it to Canada for subsequent use in the Bruce nuclear power plant. Also under study was the possibility of fabricating MOX fuel for CANDU reactors using the DEMOX facility being developed under the Russian-French-German project (see page 66 for more on the project). This could significantly reduce the total costs. According to preliminary estimates, the implementation cost of the project—targeted to burn all Russian excess plutonium only in CANDU reactors—may be $2 billion.

In addition, MINATOM, the Ministry of Foreign Affairs and External Trade of Canada, and the U.S. DOE—with U.S. and Canadian financial support—agreed to carry out the Parallex experiment, which plans for parallel irradiation in a CANDU reactor (the Chalk River nuclear power plant) of experimental MOX fuel fabricated with weapons-grade plutonium of both U.S. and Russian origin. This will enable the comparison of fuel operational characteristics. In 1999–2000, the fuel in the form of fuel rods was fabricated at the Los Alamos National Laboratory in the United States and at the Bochvar Institute in Russia. The content of weapons-grade plutonium in the Russian fuel rods was about 600 g. The pilot charge of this fuel was placed in the reactor in early 2001.[125] If the experiment and its industrial implementation are successful, Canadian experts believe that this would allow the disposal of 1.5 tons of weapons-grade plutonium per reactor per year.

COOPERATION BETWEEN RUSSIA AND JAPAN. After the Moscow nuclear security summit, Japan expressed interest in cooperating with Russia in the area of surplus weapons-grade plutonium disposition. Long-term plans for nuclear power development in Japan provide for the widespread use of fast neutron reactors. Japan, therefore, is especially interested in the Russian BN-600 reactor, which uses vibropacked MOX fuel with unique technical characteristics.[126]

The JNC Corporation, designated to take the lead in implementing the project, has developed the following three-stage work plan for interaction with the Russian side:

- Stage one (until 2003): Fabrication of three vibropacked MOX-fuel assemblies at the RIAR facility (Dimitrovgrad) and the experimental irradiation assemblies in the BN-600 reactor;

- Stage two (until 2006): Design and development of a hybrid core for the BN-600 (20 percent MOX-fuel core charge); replacement of the uranium 238 radial

---

125. A. Aleksandrov and K. Leonov, "New Stage in Plutonium Disposition Program," Atompressa, February 1, 2001.

126. Rybachenkov, "On International Cooperation of Russia in the Field of Disposition of Surplus Weapons Plutonium."

blanket with a reflector to stop production of weapons-grade plutonium; and increase the RIAR facility output capacity to meet the requirement of producing a hybrid core charge comprising 40–50 fuel assemblies per year; and

■ Stage three (until 2010): Conversion of the BN-600 core for a full MOX-fuel core charge; development of a facility with a production capacity of 250 vibro-packed MOX-fuel assemblies a year; and carry out work to extend the BN-600 reactor service life from 2010 until 2020.

COOPERATION BETWEEN RUSSIA AND THE UNITED STATES. Cooperation between Russia and the United States in the field of disposing of surplus weapons-grade plutonium started in 1994. At a meeting held in January 1994, Boris Yeltsin and Bill Clinton charged the Russian and U.S. experts "to study options for the long-term disposition of fissile materials, particularly of plutonium, taking into account the issues of nonproliferation, environmental protection, safety, and technical and economic factors."[127] The first joint report of the expert groups was published in September 1996. The most applicable plutonium disposition techniques were its immobilization and use as nuclear reactor fuel.[128] On July 24, 1998, Sergei Kirienko, then prime minister of Russia, and Al Gore, then vice president of the United States, signed an intergovernmental agreement concerning scientific and technical cooperation in the management of plutonium withdrawn from nuclear military programs. In this agreement, Russia and the United States announced their intent to

■ Continue cooperation in small-scale testing and in demonstrations of plutonium management; and

■ As soon as practically feasible, move to pilot-industrial demonstrations of plutonium management technologies.

The main areas of cooperation between Russia and the United States were announced:

■ Convert metal plutonium into oxide usable for fabrication of MOX fuel for different nuclear power reactors;

■ Stabilize unstable forms of plutonium;

■ Use plutonium as MOX fuel in different nuclear power reactors;

■ Immobilize plutonium in waste and difficult-to-reprocess forms; and

■ Dispose of immobilized plutonium containing materials in geologic repositories.

The joint coordinating committee has set up working groups to carry out the practical implementation of the agreement (see table 3.6), including:[129]

---

127. Joint U.S.-Russian Plutonium Disposition Steering Committee, "Joint United States/Russian Plutonium Disposition Study" (Washington, D.C.: U.S. Department of Energy, September 1996).

128. Ibid.

Table 3.6. U.S.-Russia Technical Cooperation in Weapons Plutonium Disposition

Area of cooperation	Russian participants
Conversion of metal plutonium; Assistance in the design and construction of a facility to convert metal plutonium into plutonium oxide usable as MOX-fuel	Bochvar Institute, RIAR, GSPI, PO Mayak, and the Scientific and Engineering Center
Development of a MOX-fuel fabrication technique; Fuel tests and certification for use in VVER and BN-600 reactors	Bochvar Institute, RIAR, JSC Novosibirsk Chemical Concentrates Plant, Atomenergo-proekt, Russian Research Center (RRC) Kurchatov Institute, the Balakovo nuclear power plant (NPP), and All-Russian Research Institute of Nuclear Power Plants (VNIIAES)
Assessment of the possibility of modifying the BN-600 reactor to dispose of plutonium	RIAR, PO Mayak, IPPE, Special Design Bureau for Mechanical Engineering (OKBM), and the Beloyarsk NPP
Study the possibility of using Canadian CANDU reactors to irradiate (burn) MOX fuel containing weapons-grade plutonium	Bochvar Institute
Development of a high-temperature gas-cooled reactor to expand plutonium disposition capabilities	Bochvar Institute, RRC Kurchatov Institute, OKBM, NPO Luch, Siberian Chemical Combine, and Novosibirsk State Design Research Institute VNIPIET
Development of plutonium immobilization technologies at Russian facilities	Bochvar Institute, GSPI, PO Mayak, Mountain Chemical Combine (MCC), VNIPIET, VNIPI Promtechnologii, and the Khlopin Institute

Source: Wolfsthal et al., *Nuclear Status Report.*

■ Conversion of metal plutonium (including scientific and technical work to support design and construction of a facility to convert metal plutonium into plutonium oxide usable for MOX fuel);

■ Light-water (thermal) reactors (including the study of issues associated with the irradiation of MOX fuel in VVER-1000 reactors and the development of fabrication technology for such fuel); the fabrication of fuel pellets for experimental fuel assemblies; and research in reactor physics and thermal hydraulics related to the transitioning from uranium to MOX fuel;

---

129. Rybachenkov, "On International Cooperation of Russia in the Field of Disposition of Surplus Weapons Plutonium."

■ Fast neutron reactors (including the development of an integrated stage-by-stage conversion plan for the BN-600 reactor; first to have a hybrid core and, eventually, a full core charged with MOX fuel);

■ Immobilization (including studies on plutonium immobilization in glass and ceramic matrices and on immobilization of plutonium-containing waste at MINATOM's industrial sites);

■ Economics, regulations and licensing; and

■ Technologies associated with high-temperature gas-cooled reactors.

To eliminate a duplication of efforts in different areas of the international assistance to Russia, a document was signed in 1999 stating the principles of coordination and scientific and technical information exchange between the U.S. DOE, the French Commissariat for Atomic Energy, Germany's Federal Foreign Office, and MINATOM. Observers from France, Germany, and Japan are regularly invited to the U.S.-Russian joint coordinating committee meetings.[130]

On September 2, 1998, the presidents of the Russian Federation and the United States signed a statement on the principles of management and disposition of plutonium designated as no longer required for defense purposes:

■ Russia and the United States will each convert approximately 50 tons of plutonium, withdrawn in stages from nuclear military programs, into forms unusable for nuclear weapons; interim storage for this material will be required;

■ The two governments will cooperate in pursuit of this goal through the consumption of plutonium fuel in existing nuclear reactors (or in reactors that may enter into service during the duration of this cooperation) or by the immobilization of the plutonium in glass or ceramic form mixed with high-level RW;

■ Russia and the United States expect that the management and disposition of this plutonium will be broadly based and multilateral, and they welcome close cooperation and coordination with other countries, including those of the G-8;

■ In cooperation with other states, Russia and the United States will, as soon as practically feasible and according to a time frame to be negotiated by the two governments, develop and operate an initial set of large-scale facilities for the conversion of the plutonium, which will be used as fuel in the above-mentioned existing reactors;

■ Conditions for the plutonium management and disposition projects will be determined by mutual consent between the parties participating in those projects;

■ In the plutonium management and disposition effort, Russia and the United States will seek to develop acceptable methods and technologies for transparency measures, including appropriate international verification measures and stringent standards for physical protection, control, and accounting for the plutonium;

---

130. Ibid.

■ For this effort to be carried out, it will be necessary to agree upon appropriate financial arrangements; and

■ Both sides will develop strategies for the management and disposition of plutonium based on the principles set forth in the July 1998 agreement as well as the bilateral agreement. They will initiate negotiation of this bilateral agreement promptly and with the intention of concluding the agreement by the end of this calendar year.

Negotiations were conducted during 1999 and 2000 and were concluded on August 31 and September 1, 2000, with the signing of an intergovernmental agreement concerning the disposition of plutonium designated as no longer required for defense purposes. The agreement creates the foundation for further cooperation between Russia and the United States regarding the disposal of the surplus weapons plutonium.

The most important provisions are:

■ Russia and the United States agreed on the disposition (conversion into a form unusable for nuclear weapons) of no less than 34 metric tons of weapons-grade plutonium;

■ Reprocessing of irradiated MOX fuel is prohibited until each side disposes of 34 tons of weapons-grade plutonium under this agreement;

■ Each side commits to start negotiating with the IAEA on the possibility of having IAEA inspections for verification of the agreement implementation;

■ Both sides will ensure the safe and secure storage of the disposed plutonium through efficient control and accounting of the plutonium as well as the application of reliable physical protection arrangements; and

■ Russia will be assured of technical and financial assistance in implementing the program.

Operation of facilities "necessary to the disposition of no less than 2 metric tons a year of its disposition plutonium" will start before December 31, 2007. Russia will follow this commitment provided it receives assistance in implementing the disposal schedule as agreed to in the agreement.

The agreement requires ratification but has been in force since its signing.[131] There have been some substantial problems during the implementation of this agreement. Russia considers weapons-grade plutonium a national treasure and a valuable power source. Therefore, the reactor option—weapons-grade plutonium is used as fuel for nuclear power reactors—has been chosen for the disposal of all Russian plutonium.

The United States initially selected two options: reactor burn and immobilization (vitrification). This raised certain concerns in Russia. Because Russian specialists believe that vitrification cannot rule out later separation of the plutonium, the principle of irreversibility is breached and threatens the nonproliferation

---

131. "There are 124 governmental draft laws on the State Duma review," Russian Information Agency Novosti, March 21, 2002.

Table 3.7. U.S. Funding for Russian Implementation of U.S.-Russia Agreement

Program	Funds	Schedule
Design of industrial-scale facilities	Up to $70 million	2000–2003
Construction of industrial-scale facilities	Up to $130 million	2003–2007

Source: "Agreement between the Government of the United States of America and the Government of the Russian Federation Concerning Disposition and Management of Plutonium Designated as No Longer Required for Defense Purposes and Related Cooperation," September 1, 2000, p. 29, www.nti.org/db/nisprofs/russia/fulltext/plutdisp/pudispft.pdf.

regime.[132] In January 2002, DOE announced that it had discarded the immobilization option and had chosen instead to use only the MOX-fuel option for the management of surplus weapons-grade plutonium. This would save up to $2 billion regarding implementation of the U.S. part of the program.[133]

The major difficulties encountered were in regard to financing the Russian side of the program. Many Russian experts believe that even the access and the agreement implementation verification issues can be easily resolved, provided that funding is available.[134] The cost of implementing the Russian weapons-grade plutonium disposition program is about $2 billion for 20 years, not including the cost of management and transparency arrangements.[135]

In July 2000, the leaders of the G-8 countries agreed that an expert group would have to prepare a decision on financing the Russian side of the plutonium disposition program before the 2001 G-8 summit.[136] This goal was not met, however. The United States, the United Kingdom, Japan, and France announced their decision to set aside $600 million in funding.[137] At the Canadian G-8 summit in June 2002, it was decided to finance a wide range of nonproliferation programs in Russia— including plutonium disposition. Also being considered is the possibility of commercializing the program: power-generating companies in countries interested in disarmament (such as Germany, Switzerland, Sweden, Belgium, Japan, and others) could use MOX fuel containing Russian weapons-grade plutonium.[138] Proposals have been made recently to involve private power-generating companies in the dis-

---

132. Rybachenkov, "On International Cooperation of Russia in the Field of Disposition of Surplus Weapons Plutonium."

133. "Secretary Abraham Announces Administration Plan to Proceed with Plutonium Disposition & Reduce Proliferation Concerns," press release no. PR-02-007, U.S. Department of Energy, January 23, 2002, www.energy.gov/HQPress/releases02/janpr/pr02007.htm.

134. Valentin Ivanov, first deputy minister of MINATOM, "On Implementation of International Agreements Concerning Disposition of Plutonium Designated as No Longer Required for Defense Purposes and Problems Associated with its Management" (report to Russian Federation government meeting, press center of the Russian Federation, February 8, 2001).

135. Ibid.

136. Disposition of U.S. and Russian Federation Weapon-grade Plutonium, Fact Sheet, G-8 Economic Summit 2000, Office of the Press Secretary, The White House, July 21, 2000, www.state.gov/www/issues/economic/summit/000721_whfs_plutonium.html.

137. Comments of Russian program participants during roundtable discussion at the PIR Center, March 6, 2002.

Table 3.8. Estimated Annual Funding Requirements for Fissile Materials Disposition Program, 2002–2008, millions of U.S. dollars

	2002[a]	2003[b]	2004	2005	2006	2007	2008
Total	19.0	34.0	48.6	66.7	68.4	70.4	72.5
Including in Russia	6.0	20.0	32.4	44.4	45.6	47.0	48.4
Including in the U.S.	13.0	14.0	16.2	22.2	22.8	23.5	24.2

Source: "Report to Congress: Disposition of Surplus Defense Plutonium at the Savannah River Site" (Washington, D.C.: National Nuclear Security Administration, Office of Fissile Materials Disposition, February 15, 2002), p. ES-5, table ES-6.

a. Allocated.

b. Budget request from U.S. DOE.

position of surplus weapons-grade plutonium by providing them with tax exemptions and other disarmament-related benefits.[139]

In accordance with the U.S.-Russia Plutonium Management and Disposition Agreement, the United States committed itself to the allocation of $200 million for implementation of the Russian side of the program (table 3.7).

In February 2002, the DOE published estimates regarding additional funds to finance the Russian side of the program in 2002–2008 (table 3.8).

U.S.-Russia HEU-LEU Conversion Program

In February 1993, Russia and the United States signed an intergovernmental agreement concerning the use of HEU removed from nuclear weapons. They agreed that 500 tons of Russian HEU with more than 90 percent enrichment of uranium 235 content that is removed from nuclear weapons would be blended down into LEU (not more than 20 percent enrichment for uranium 235) and sold in the United States to be used in U.S. power reactors. Initially it was planned that Russia would be paid $12 billion within 20 years for the LEU, but later the LEU price was tied to the market price. That will possibly reduce the total sum Russia will receive. When they signed the intergovernmental agreement, both sides agreed that:

■ The agreed rate for the blending down of HEU into LEU would be 10 tons per year during the first five years of the agreement and 30 tons in each subsequent year;

■ Uranium transferred to the United States would be used exclusively for peaceful purposes;

■ Uranium supplied to the United States would be placed under the IAEA safeguards; and

138. Ivanov, "On Implementation of International Agreements Concerning Disposition of Plutonium."

139. Brent Scowcroft and Daniel Poneman, "From Plutonium to Plowshares," *Los Angeles Times*, October 31, 2001, http://ffip.com/plutonium/.

■ Under this agreement the nuclear materials would be provided with physical protection at a level not less than that recommended by the IAEA (INFCIRC/225/REV.2).

Tekhsnabexport was designated as the executive body by the Russian side and the United States Enrichment Corporation (USEC) was designated by the U.S. side. At the time of the signing, the USEC was a federally managed company, but it was privatized in 1996.

The main problem in implementing the agreement was the issue of payment for the feed component of the LEU being delivered. According to the contract, the LEU price is determined to be the sum of two components:

■ Cost of enrichment/downblending (about 2/3 of the contract price); and

■ Cost of the feed component (about 1/3 of the contract price).

It was agreed that the USEC would pay for the enrichment services within 60 days of delivery, but would pay for the feed component after the LEU had been sold on the U.S. market or used at USEC facilities. The 1996 USEC privatization legislation stated that the U.S. corporation, following receipt of LEU from Russia, was obligated to transfer to Tekhsnabexport natural uranium equivalent to the amount present in the material delivered from Russia. Tekhsnabexport could then sell the received natural uranium on the world market. However, Tekhsnabexport was unable to sell the natural uranium at a suitable price, and this led to the suspension of the HEU-LEU deal three times. A portion of material that remained unsold by Tekhsnabexport was then bought by DOE in order to resume implementation of the contract. In late February 2002, Tekhsnabexport and the USEC reached a new agreement: in the future the price would not be fixed but would be dependent on world market prices.[140]

To verify that the HEU being supplied to the USEC comes from dismantled nuclear warheads, the United States carries out inspections at the facilities involved in implementing the HEU-LEU agreement. MINATOM's commercial interests have forced it to agree to a more intrusive inspection mechanism than those carried out under other U.S.-Russia projects. In turn, MINATOM carries out inspections at U.S. facilities to verify peaceful uses of the LEU supplied to the United States. The importance of this program and, respectively, the monitoring of its implementation, is witnessed by the fact that from 1994 to 2001 DOE spent $89 million on transparency measures.

As of September 2002, about 140 tons of HEU have been blended down under the HEU-LEU agreement (table 3.9). That is equal to 5,665 eliminated warheads. Russia was paid about $2.5 billion.

Professionals involved in the nuclear market, consumers in that market, and the U.S. administration are currently questioning USEC policies. The USEC's economic instability may lead to a reduction in the number of deliveries of Russian LEU, which currently fulfills about 50 percent of the U.S. demand for nuclear fuel.

---

140. Ivan Lebedev, "Agreement Reached on New Conditions of Contract to Supply Russian Uranium to the USA," ITAR-TASS, February 24, 2002.

Table 3.9. Blend Down of HEU into LEU under the HEU-LEU Agreement, in metric tons

	1995	1996	1997	1998	1999	2000	2001	2002
HEU blended down	6	12	18	14.5	21.3	30	30	8.5
LEU delivered	186	371	480	450	624	858	904	244

Source: United States Enrichment Corporation, "Status Report, U.S.-Russian Megatons to Megawatts Program," www.usec.com/v2001_02/HTML/Megatons_status.asp.

Recently there has been discussion in the United States about replacing the USEC as executive agent or expanding the number of executive agents.

Measures proposed to improve the efficiency of the HEU-LEU deal include doubling the speed of the downblending rate for the uranium (which has already been paid for) and storing the downblended uranium in Russia without putting it on the market (and thus destabilizing it).[141] In spite of the difficulties this would cause, it is hard to overestimate the significance of this issue for Russia. The money received through implementation of the deal makes up a significant part of MINATOM's budget and pays for a number of important MINATOM programs targeted for restructuring the nuclear weapons complex and the creation of new jobs.

U.S.-Russia Cooperation for Plutonium Production Reactor Conversion

On June 23, 1994, the governments of Russia and the United States signed an agreement regarding the shutdown of operating plutonium production reactors and halting the use of newly produced plutonium for nuclear weapons. Russia has not been fulfilling its part of the agreement, however, because its three existing plutonium production reactors[142] are the source for heat and electricity in nearby cities. On September 23, 1997, the government of the Russian Federation and the government of the United States signed an agreement concerning cooperation regarding the plutonium production reactors. In accordance with the agreement, the three reactors still operating would be modified and would cease production of "non-reactor plutonium" by December 31, 2000. The U.S. side, as much as possible, would provide for adequate financing of joint work to carry out the necessary modifications.

This agreement has run into trouble. MINATOM blames the trouble on a breach of the financing schedule.[143] The problems, however, may have been MINA-

---

141. Kenneth N. Luongo, "Options for Increased U.S.-Russian Nuclear Nonproliferation Cooperation and Projected Costs" (Washington, D.C.: RANSAC, October 2001), www.ransac.org/new-web-site/pub/reports/options_paper_101101.html.

142. Two reactors are in Seversk (formerly Tomsk-7) and one reactor is in Zheleznogorsk (formerly Krasnoyarsk-26).

143. Yekaterina Kats, "Poverty Is the Enemy of Conversion: Russia Will Produce More Weapons-Grade Plutonium," *Vremya novostei*, August 28, 2001.

TOM's fault. MINATOM had delayed selecting an option for discontinuing weapons-grade plutonium production: either reactor core conversion, halting production of weapons-grade plutonium, or replacement of the nuclear power plant with a fossil fuel plant. In August 2001, Russia and the United States signed a protocol to the 1997 agreement to allow plutonium production at reactors in Seversk and Zheleznogorsk until December 31, 2006. The protocol anticipated two options: nuclear and nonnuclear. However, eventually it was decided that all three existing reactors should be replaced with fossil-fuel power plants.[144]

---

144. Vladimir Rybachenkov (comments during roundtable discussion at the PIR Center, March 6, 2002).

CHAPTER 4

Destruction of Russia's Chemical Weapons

Russia inherited from the disintegrated USSR the world's largest stockpile—some 40,000 tons—of CW agents, located at seven storage facilities and twenty-four fabrication, assembly, and charging facilities.

Russian officials have stated that the production of CW ceased in 1987. But the CW elimination plant built in the late 1980s in Chapaevsk (Samara region) never began operations because of massive protests by the local population, who feared severe environmental contamination.

In the 1990s, Russia did not begin large-scale elimination of CW, explaining that it did not have the financial resources to build the costly facilities and necessary industrial and social infrastructure. In 1993, when it signed the Chemical Weapons Convention, Moscow made the implementation of the convention subject to significant amounts of external assistance. External assistance of more than $290 million received by mid-2001 as well as R1,265 million (in 2001 prices) budgeted by the Russian Federation proved to be far from sufficient to begin the elimination of the chemical arsenal. In addition, the start of CW elimination was delayed because of poorly tested technology for the safe destruction of large amounts of CW agents and chaotic decisionmaking, including a lack of coordination of activities by the agencies involved. A 1997 paper issued by the State Duma Committee for Industry, Construction, Transport, and Power Engineering stated:

> Any kind of system for RF Government decisionmaking, supervision over the fulfillment of project goals, and the coordination of efforts by the agencies participating in the program implementation, is lacking.[145]

The failure of Russia to fulfill its commitments regarding the convention will devalue this important component of arms control and may trigger the proliferation of CW. For Russia itself, this would mean a shameful degradation of its international profile and a simultaneous increase in the risk of large-scale ecological catastrophes. Particularly serious is the fact that two thirds of the Russian chemical arsenal (about 27,000 tons) is stored in the Volga basin. Speaking to the State Duma in 1997, A. Kvashnin, chief of general staff, stressed:

---

145. "State Duma Committee for Industry, Construction, Transport and Power Engineering (comments and recommendations concerning the federal draft law, 'On Ratification of the Convention on the Prohibition of the Development, Production, and Stockpiling of Chemical Weapons and on Their Destruction')," *Chemical Weapons and Problems of Their Elimination* (in Russian) No. 5 (Spring–Summer 1998): 15.

Table 4.1. Russian Stockpiles of Category 1 Chemical Weapons, 2002

Chemical agent	Amount (thousand tons)	Share (%)
Nerve agents (sarin, soman, VX)	32.2	80
Blister agents (mustard, lewisite, and their mixtures)	7.8	20

Source: Russian Munitions Agency, "Stockpiles of Chemical Weapons in the Russian Federation,"
   http://www.munition.gov.ru/eng/zapasho.html.

Even the freshest stockpiles of chemical weapons have been on the shelf for more than 10 years. A batch of vesicants was produced in the '40s…. They pose a potential environmental threat to the population and environment, especially in the case of natural disasters or emergencies. The chemical weapons storage facilities…are located in heavily populated regions. Settlements built near chemical warfare arsenals have grown too close…. Chemical weapons cannot be stored at the guaranteed level of security for an unlimited period of time. One should bear in mind that, without overdramatizing it, we have less and less time until the moment comes when the chemical munitions start leaking in mass. Therefore, it is dangerous to delay the elimination of these weapons.[146]

The danger of an ecological catastrophe may increase significantly during the currently planned shipment of munitions containing nearly 6,000 tons of organophosphorus CW agents from Kizner to Shchuch'ye for their destruction.

Any immediate danger of the proliferation of CW during long-term storage in the Russian chemical arsenals is relatively low. Official sources state that all CW are concentrated in storage facilities with sufficient security levels. These storage facilities are located in small settlements where access is effectively controlled. Theft followed by long-distance shipment within Russia of chemical munitions or CW agents in more or less traceable quantities seems unrealistic.

The failure of Russia to fulfill the major requirements of the CWC might trigger other states to disregard or reject the CWC. It is also important that sensitive information associated with the Russian chemical arsenal and its production centers should not reach countries of concern or terrorist organizations that are seeking to create CW of their own.

Russian Chemical Stockpile

About 80 percent of the CW stockpiles in Russia are organophosphorus nerve agents (sarin, soman, and VX); the others are vesicants (mustard gas, lewisite, and their mixtures). They make up category 1 chemical weapons. Chemical agents are in artillery shells, gravity bombs, and tactical missile warheads (except for mustard gas and 60 percent of the stockpile of lewisite, both of which are stored in tanks).

---

146. Ibid., 7.

Table 4.2. Location of Russia's Chemical Weapons

Storage site	Percent of stockpile	Volume[a] (tons)	Chemical agent
Kambarka, Udmurtia	15.9	6,360	Blister agents
Gorny, Saratov region	2.9	1,160	Blister agents
Kizner, Udmurtia	14.2	5,680	Nerve agents
Pochep, Bryansk region	18.8	7,520	Nerve agents
Shchuch'ye, Kurgan region	13.6	5,440	Nerve agents
Maradykovsky, Kirov region	17.4	6,960	Nerve agents
Leonidovka, Penza region	17.2	6,880	Nerve agents

Source: Russian Munitions Agency, "Resolution of July 5, 2001, No. 510, On Introduction of Amendments and Supplements to Resolution of the Government of the Russian Federation of March 21, 1996, No. 305, 'On approval of Federal Target Programme Destruction of Chemical Weapons Stockpiles in the Russian Federation,'" Appendix 2, "List of Chemical Weapons Storage Facilities Locations" (in Russian), www.munition.gov.ru/eng/objects.html.

a. The volume has been calculated from a Russian stockpile of 40,000 tons.

This substantially complicates the CW elimination process since it is necessary to open up and process several million munitions. Russian experts estimate that the detoxification stage for the chemical agents takes up no more than 5 percent of the destruction process; the rest is for the demilitarization of the munitions, processing and deactivation of their shells, cleanup of discharges and drains, standard and off-normal decontamination, destruction of packages, safety insurance, and the prevention of accidents.[147]

Phosgene is a category 2 chemical weapon. Unequipped chemical munitions, explosives related to category 3 chemical weapons, as well as phosgene and phosgene-equipped shells were eliminated in Russia by the summer of 2002 (table 4.1).

Munitions charged with nerve agents are stored at five large facilities, each housing approximately 5.5 to 7.5 tons of CW agents (table 4.2). The main storage location of blister agents is at the facility near Kambarka (Udmurt republic). In addition, about 1,200 tons of chemical agents are located in a facility near the village of Gorny (Saratov region).

The CWC also provides for the elimination or conversion of CW facilities that produce munitions to deliver CW agents to targets, the CW agents themselves, and facilities where munitions are charged with the chemical agents. The elimination or conversion of a total of 24 facilities is planned; six were eliminated by the summer of 2001. All special equipment was dismantled in nine of them, and the rest were partially dismantled or converted (table 4.3). The main CW production centers of

147. Viktor Petrunin, "Technological Approaches to Elimination of Chemical Weapons," *Chemical Weapons and Problems of Their Elimination* (in Russian) No. 1 (Spring 1996): 18.

Table 4.3. Russia's CW Production Facilities, May 2001

Type	Number of facilities	Status
CW agents and CW precursor production	14	Physically destroyed: 4 100% of special equipment destroyed: 4 75% of special equipment destroyed: 1 To be destroyed, converted, or dismantled: 5
Nonchemical components of CW munitions assemblies	2	100% of special equipment destroyed: 1 Partly destroyed, partly subject to conversion: 1
Loading of munitions	8	Physically destroyed: 2 Conversion accomplished: 1 100% of special equipment destroyed: 4 Partly converted, partly destroyed: 1

Source: Russian Munitions Agency, "Resolution of July 5, 2001, No. 510, On Introduction of Amendments and Supplements to Resolution of the Government of the Russian Federation of March 21, 1996, No. 305, 'On approval of Federal Target Programme Destruction of Chemical Weapons Stockpiles in the Russian Federation,'" Appendix 3, "List of Chemical Weapons Production Facilities Subject to Conversion or Destruction" (in Russian), www.munition.gov.ru/eng/36.html.

the former Soviet Union were located in the Volga basin. They included Volgograd, eight facilities; Dzerzhinsk (Nizhegolodskaya region), seven facilities; Novochebok-sarsk (Chuvashiya), five facilities; Chapaevsk (Samara region), three facilities; and Berezniki (Perm region), one facility.

Timeline for CW Destruction

Russia's chemical weapons are to be destroyed in accordance with the CWC time schedule:

- Not less than two years after the convention enters into force,[148] the testing of the first destruction facility shall be completed;

- Not less than 1 percent of category 1 chemical weapons[149] shall be destroyed no later than three years after the convention enters into force;

- Not less than 20 percent of category 1 chemical weapons shall be destroyed no later than five years after the convention enters into force;

- Not less than 45 percent of category 1 chemical weapons shall be destroyed no later than seven years after the convention enters into force;

---

148. For Russia, the convention entered into force in 1997.

■ All category 1 chemical weapons shall be destroyed no later than 10 years after the convention enters into force;

■ The destruction of category 2 chemical weapons shall start no later than one year after the convention enters into force, and the complete destruction shall be no later than five years after the convention enters force; and

■ The destruction of category 3 chemical weapons shall start no later than one year after the convention enters into force, and the complete destruction shall be not later than five years after the convention enters into force.

The CWC also contains the clause that, if a state believes that it will be unable to ensure the destruction of its chemical weapons in accordance to the above schedule, it may request that the executive council of the Organization for Prohibition of Chemical Weapons (OPCW) recommend to the conference of the OPCW an extension of its obligations. The request should contain:

■ The duration of the proposed extension;

■ A detailed explanation of the reasons for the proposed extension; and

■ A detailed plan for destruction during the proposed extension and the remaining portion of the original 10-year period for destruction.

A decision on the request shall be taken by the conference at its next session on the recommendation of the executive council. Any extension shall be the minimum necessary, but in no case should the deadline for a state to complete its destruction of all CW be extended beyond 15 years after the entry into force of the convention.

For Russia, this means that the final date for the total destruction of its chemical weapons is the year 2012.

Russia's Chemical Weapons Destruction Program

By the summer of 2002, Russia had eliminated chemical weapons in categories 2 and 3 in the facilities at Maradykovsky and Leonidovka, but elimination of chemical weapons in category 1 has not yet began.

Russia signed the CWC in 1993, and it was ratified by the Duma in 1997. On March 21, 1996, the government of the Russian Federation approved the federal special program called "Destruction of Chemical Weapons Stockpiles in the Rus-

---

149. Category 1 chemicals are high-risk chemicals that have little or no use except for purposes prohibited by the CWC; they are developed, produced, stockpiled, or used as a chemical weapon (as defined in Article II of the CWC); possess a chemical structure closely related to that of other toxic chemicals; and could be used as a chemical weapon or as a precursor of a toxic chemical. Category 2 chemicals are significant-risk chemicals; they may be used as precursors; and they are not produced in large commercial quantities for uses sanctioned under the CWC. Category 3 chemicals are those that have been produced, stockpiled, or used as chemical weapons, that could be lethal or incapacitating, and that could be important in the production of category 1 or 2 chemicals. Category 3 chemicals, however, can be produced in large commercial quantities for purposes not prohibited by the CWC. See http://projects.sipri.se/cbw/docs/cw-cwc-chemannexA.html.

**Table 4.4. Renewed Schedule of CW Elimination Program, Category 1 and
Category 2 Chemicals, July 2001, in metric tons, cumulative**

2001	2002	2003	2004	2005	2006	2007	2008	2009	2010	2011
5	195	585	975	2,125	5,805	12,365	20,365	28,365	36,365	40,000

Source: Russian Munitions Agency, "Resolution of July 5, 2001, No. 510, On Introduction of
Amendments and Supplements to Resolution of the Government of the Russian Federation of
March 21, 1996, No. 305, 'On approval of Federal Target Programme Destruction of Chemical
Weapons Stockpiles in the Russian Federation,'" Appendix 4, "Amounts and Schedules for
Destruction of Category 1 and Category 2 Chemical Weapons" (in Russian), www.muni-
tion.gov.ru/eng/36.html.

sian Federation," which set out the plan that all CW stockpiles and their production
facilities were to be eliminated under the international monitoring regime by no
later than 2007. To accomplish this, the government planned to build seven facilities for the destruction of CW. The four-year gap between the signing and
ratification of the CWC was caused by both political and economic factors. Some in
the Russian military command and left-wing political elite expressed doubts about
the rationale for the elimination of Russia's chemical arsenal. Other causes were
more substantial, however: a lack of budgeted funds, the difficulty of choosing an
environmentally safe technique for the destruction of large amounts of CW, and
general organizational disorder.

Russia found itself in a position of being incapable of implementing its own
decisions and plans for CW elimination. The difficult economic situation in the
country, the lack of financial resources, and insufficient external assistance all
played their roles. In 1999, the U.S. Congress terminated assistance to Russia that
had been targeted for the elimination of CW; one of the reasons given was the
doubt about Russia's capability to meet its obligations under the convention within
the acceptable terms. This perceived inability was attributed to Russia's reluctance
or inability to allocate necessary funds. Russia felt seriously threatened that it would
not meet its obligations under the CWC and therefore would have to face unfavor-
able economic and political consequences.

As a result, Russia intensified its efforts to prepare for CW elimination. In 2000,
the CW elimination responsibilities were transferred from the Ministry of Defense
to the Russian Munitions Agency. In 2001, the State Commission on Chemical Disarmament was created. In 2001, federal appropriations for chemical disarmament
increased six times compared with 2000, and in 2002 they are to double[150] and
approach R5.4 billion.[151] Russia's contribution together with foreign financial assis-

---

150. Sergei Kirienko, interview (in Russian), ITAR-TASS, February 21, 2002.

151. "The Russian and U.S. President Summit May Consider Issue of Chemical Weapons
Stockpiles Elimination" (in Russian), ITAR-TASS, March 5, 2002.

Table 4.5. Comparison of 1996 and 2001 Federal Special Programs for Destruction of CW in Russian Federation

Functions	1996 program	2001 program
Obligations under the CWC	Elimination of chemical stockpiles	Elimination of chemical stockpiles, elimination and/or conversion of CW production facilities, international inspection, national implementation of the CWC
Duration of program	1995–2009	2001–2012
Construction of CW elimination facilities	7 facilities; all were planned to accomplish the full cycle of CW elimination	3 facilities; existing industrial facilities are planned to be involved in CW elimination
Transport of chemical weapons	Not planned	Plan to transport organophosphorus agents to elimination facility in Shchuch'ye, among others
Infrastructure	Planned to provide facilities staff with permanent residences	Social infrastructure expenditures are minimized

Source: Russian Munitions Agency, "Resolution of July 5, 2001, No. 510, On Introduction of Amendments and Supplements to Resolution of the Government of the Russian Federation of March 21, 1996, No. 305, 'On approval of Federal Target Programme Destruction of Chemical Weapons Stockpiles in the Russian Federation,'" www.munition.gov.ru/eng/36.html.

tance comes to approximately R9 billion.[152] In 2002, Russia also needed about $120 million from abroad to arrive at a budget of R9 billion.

In July 2001, the Russian government approved amendments to the 1996 program for destruction of chemical weapons stockpiles in Russia; the amendments provide for the process to be completed by 2011 (table 4.4). After a review of the CW elimination strategy and to reduce costs, it was decided to build three full-scale CW elimination facilities instead of seven, only two of which (in the city of Shchuch'ye in Kurgan region and in the city of Kambarka in Udmurtia) will be able to process the CW agents through to final destruction. In the village of Gorny (Saratov region), where the elimination of chemical weapons currently in storage is to take place, the construction of a vesicant CW agent elimination facility will be

---

152. "Sergei Kirienko to discuss issues related to funding of Russian Chemical Weapons Elimination Program at upcoming meeting with Dick Cheney" (in Russian), ITAR-TASS, January 23, 2002.

Table 4.6. CW Destruction Process in Russia, July 2001

Location	Mission	Period of operation
Gorny	Destruction of blister agents	2002–2005
Kambarka	Destruction of blister agents	2005–2011
Shchuch'ye	Destruction of nerve agents	2005–2011
Maradykovsky	Demilitarization and detoxification	2006–2011
Pochep	Demilitarization and detoxification	2006–2011
Leonidovka	Demilitarization and detoxification	2006–2011
Kizner	Transportation to Shchuch'ye for destruction	Before 2012

Source: Russian Munitions Agency, "Resolution of July 5, 2001, No. 510, On Introduction of Amendments and Supplements to Resolution of the Government of the Russian Federation of March 21, 1996, No. 305, 'On approval of Federal Target Programme Destruction of Chemical Weapons Stockpiles in the Russian Federation,'" www.munition.gov.ru/eng/36.html.

completed. Three other small-capacity facilities (in Pochep, Maradykovsky, and Leonidovka) are planned for the "demilitarization" of munitions and detoxification—reprocessing to a less toxic substance—of organophosphorus CW agents. After detoxification they can be stored, transported, and ultimately disposed of at other facilities until 2012. Nerve CW agents, stored in Kizner, are slated for relocation and ultimate destruction at the facility in Shchuch'ye. See table 4.5 for a comparison of the 1996 program with the 2001 program.

Implementation of the program approved in 2001 has begun in a number of areas. In January 2002, the Gorny CW elimination facility started testing processing equipment, and it was planned to start operation in June 2002. See table 4.6 for a proposed schedule for CW destruction in Russia. In 2001, the federal budget allocated R1.5 billion (about $50 million at the current exchange rate) to complete the construction of the plant, assemble equipment, and carry out the start-up and equipment adjustment. In 2002, about R2 billion (about $65 million at the current exchange rate) will be spent on the Gorny facility.

The amended chemical weapons elimination program begun in 2001 sounds more reasonable and realistic than the program the Duma ratified in 1997; however, experts are debating several points:

■ Transportation of CW agents from Kizner to Shchuch'ye requires a review of the legislation and poses a threat of a catastrophic accident;

■ Although the United States, as the major financial contributor to the construction of the facility at Shchuch'ye, expects construction to be complete in 2007–2008 (in FY 2008), the Russians approved a program in July 2001 that expects CW elimination to begin in 2005;[153]

Table 4.7. Russian Estimates of Cost of CW Destruction, in billions of denominated rubles and U.S. dollars

	1996	1997		2001
In rubles	16.6	25.0	34.4	92.7
In U.S. dollars	3.1–3.3	4.0–4.3	5.7	3.3

Sources: *The Military Balance 1996/97* (London: Oxford University Press and International Institute for Strategic Studies, 1996), 107; *SIPRI Yearbook 2000: Armaments, Disarmament, and International Security* (in Russian) (Moscow: Nauka, 2001), 508.

Note: Both sources for this table provided the Russian estimates in rubles. The amounts in U.S. dollars were calculated according to exchange rates prevailing in the stated years.

■ Although the design capacity of the Shchuch'ye facility is 1,200 tons per year, it is planned that more than 11,000 CW agents will be eliminated there between 2005 and 2011;[154] and

■ Extensive external assistance for the undertaking is foreseen, but there are no guarantees that it will be allocated.

Costs for Russian Chemical Stockpile Destruction

It has become common practice to state that, because of Russia's economic difficulties during the transitional period, in the next decade there will not be enough resources to independently eliminate CW and CW production facilities as well as meet other obligations under the convention. Successful stockpile destruction requires a thorough analysis of the necessary costs and methodologies proposed. Even very general estimates of the costs to implement the CW elimination program presented by the Russian official agencies in the 1990s raise serious questions.

In 1996, the total cost of the federal program to eliminate chemical weapons was estimated at R16.7 billion (denominated rubles); the following year, Russian official documents and statements contained two figures: R25 billion and R34.4 billion (see table 4.7). In 2001, the expenditures were estimated at R92.7 billion. After being converted into U.S. dollars at the current exchange rate, the costs ranged from $3 billion to almost $6 billion. Such a spread of estimates, especially when expressed in U.S. dollars, cannot be explained by inflation, inaccuracies due to converting the currencies using the current exchange rate, and the like. Instead, the spread demonstrates the inadequate consideration given to accurate financial estimates for the Russian programs. This appearance of poor planning hinders external assistance.

A question arises: Are the statements true concerning the Russian inability to independently finance the elimination or a significant part of the elimination of CW? Current estimates indicate that during the next decade it will be necessary to

153. As of late 2002, the U.S. Congress had not approved the allocation of funds to build the facility in Shchuch'ye.

154. Alexander Kalyadin, "Next Chance?" *Yaderny Kontrol* (in Russian) No. 2 (March–April 2002).

spend about R93 billion—a bit over R9 billion annually (about $300 million at the exchange rate in early 2002). This is a significant amount, but it is only about 0.3 percent of Russia's annual export revenues, about 0.8 percent of the federal budget expenditures in 2001, and approximately 4.5 percent of the Russian Federation's Ministry of Defense budget in 2001.

The large discrepancy between the 1996 and 2001 program budget estimates is likely due to shoddy work done for the 1996 cost estimate, when it was planned to allocate only one-third of all available funds to the major operations—tearing down the facilities that make chemical weapons and destroying the weapons themselves as well as constructing the CW elimination facilities. For the 2001 program, budget experts drew up more realistic estimates for these major operations—closer to two-thirds of program resources.

Problems may arise, however, because in the 2001 program budget estimates only about R31 billion (or about $1 billion at the early 2002 exchange rate) have been allocated for the construction of CW elimination facilities. A single such facility—in Shchuch'ye—may cost as much as $1 billion, yet table 4.5 shows that three are planned. The U.S. DOD estimates that the total U.S. assistance needed for this project will be almost $900 million.[155] Where will the additional funds be found?

The amendments to Russia's chemical weapons elimination program that were approved by the government of Russia in July 2001 avoid linking specific amounts of internal and external funding. The program budget states only that "the volume of annual funds from the federal budget required for program implementation shall be specified annually and shall depend on the volume of financial aid made available by the country-parties of the convention and on the volume of non-budgetary funding for the program obtained from other sources."[156] One possible interpretation of this formula is that Russia will be allocating finances to eliminate CW in an amount equal to the difference between the funds envisaged by the program and funds allocated by the donor countries. (See table 4.8 for specific funding information.)

Foreign Assistance for Russia's CW Destruction Program

Many in Russia believe that external assistance is a key source of financing for the elimination of CW. Russia was anticipating approximately $1 billion from several countries (see table 4.9) from 2001 to 2006; by May 2001 about $300 million of that amount had already been spent. About 90 percent of the funding, both allocated and planned, is to be provided by the United States, which is the main donor to Russia for this project. In addition to financing the work at the Shchuch'ye facility, the United States financed equipment for the Central Laboratory for Chemical and Analytical Control (for chemical disarmament), supplied three mobile chemical

---

155. Seth Brugger, "U.S. Funding for Schuch'ye in Jeopardy," Organization for the Prohibition of Chemical Weapons, 2000, www.opcw.org/synthesis/html/s4/page_35.html.

156. Russian Munitions Agency, "Resolution of July 5, 2001, No. 510, On Introduction of Amendments and Supplements to Resolution of the Government of the Russian Federation of March 21, 1996, No. 305, 'On approval of Federal Target Programme Destruction of Chemical Weapons Stockpiles in the Russian Federation,'" www.munition.gov.ru/eng/36.html.

Table 4.8. Funding of Major Russian CW Programs, in millions of denominated rubles

Activity	1996		2001	
	Rubles	Percent	Rubles	Percent
Safety of CW storage and destruction	300	1.8	1,279	1.4
R&D in the field of CW destruction	481	2.9	2,061	2.2
Construction of CW destruction facilities	2,877	15.4	31,781	34.3
Operation of CW destruction facilities	3,018	18.1	24,877	26.8
Implementation of federal laws relating to chemical demilitarization	3,300	19.8	12,300	13.3
Other[a]	6,666	40.0	20,439	22.0
Total	16,642	100.0	92,737	100.0

Sources: "Now Russia Is Ready for Chemical Weapons Dismantlement," *Chemical Weapons and Problems of Their Elimination* (in Russian) No. 1 (Spring 1996): 2; Russian Munitions Agency, "Resolution of July 5, 2001, No. 510, On Introduction of Amendments and Supplements to Resolution of the Government of the Russian Federation of March 21, 1996, No. 305, 'On approval of Federal Target Programme Destruction of Chemical Weapons Stockpiles in the Russian Federation,'" Appendix 5, "Distribution of Funds for Major Activities under the Program" (in Russian), www.munition.gov.ru/eng/36.html.

a. Includes medical care for personnel involved in CW storage and destruction, medical and environmental monitoring, logistics and transportation, destruction of production facilities, and destruction of category 2 and category 3 chemical weapons.

laboratories for monitoring the elimination of CW, and assisted in disposing of CW at two CW production facilities (in Volgograd and Novocheboksarsk).

In 1999, the U.S. Congress terminated assistance to Russia in eliminating CW. This decision was encouraged by the 1999 publication of a General Accounting Office report[157] that seriously criticized Russian policy concerning the elimination of CW. The report noted that the planned capacity of Shchuch'ye facility—500 tons of CW agents annually—appears insufficient to meet the stated task of eliminating by 2007 5,500 tons of CW agents stored there. The report doubted that Russia would be able to—or would want to—finance other operations to eliminate CW. The GAO's concerns were realistic. If financing remains at the 1998–1999 level, Russian experts themselves note that it would take 100 years for Russia to eliminate all its CW.[158]

---

157. "Weapons of Mass Destruction: Effort to Reduce Russian Arsenals May Cost More, Achieve Less Than Planned," Report No. GAO/NSIAD-99-76 (Washington, D.C.: U.S. General Accounting Office, April 1999), 11–16.

Table 4.9. Foreign Assistance to Russia for CW Destruction, May 2001–2006, current as of 2002

Donor	Legal basis for assistance	Target of assistance	Funds
Canada	Assistance provided under agreements with the United States	Elimination of CW, Shchuch'ye	Can$100,000 ($70,000); in 2001, Can$250 million ($175 million)
European Union	Assistance provided under agreements with Germany	Elimination of CW, Gorny and Shchuch'ye	€5.8 million; €2.5–€3 million in 2001–2003
Finland	Interdepartmental Agreement, October 25, 2000	Storage of CW, Kambarka and Gorny	Fimr6 million ($1.2 million)
Germany	Framework Agreement, December 16, 1992; Interdepartmental Agreement, October 22, 1993	Elimination of CW, Gorny	DM68.0 million (approx. $27 million)
Italy	Framework Agreement, January 20, 2000	Elimination of CW, Shchuch'ye	Lit15 billion (approx. $8 million)
Netherlands	Framework Agreement, December 22, 1992	Storage of CW, Kambarka	f.25 million ($12 million)
Norway	Negotiations on agreement are under way	—	NKr9 million ($1 million) in 2001–2002
Sweden	Negotiations on agreement are under way	Storage of CW, Kambarka; equipping region's central hospital	SKr2.6 million ($700,000)
Switzerland	Negotiations on possible cooperation are under way	Elimination of CW, Kambarka and Shchuch'ye	Up to SwF50 million in 2003–2012
United Kingdom	Negotiations on agreement are under way	Elimination of CW, Shchuch'ye	£12 million ($18 million)
United States	Framework Agreement, June 17, 1992; Interdepartmental Agreement, July 30, 1993	Elimination of CW, Shchuch'ye; and Federal Institute for Organic Chemistry and Technology (GosNIIOKhT), Moscow	$286.5 million

Source: "Financial Assistance to States Donors to the Russian CW Destruction Programme," Russian Munitions Agency, www.munition.gov.ru/eng/inter.html.

In 2000, when the FY 2001 budget was being debated, the U.S. Congress formulated several conditions for the resumption of assistance to Russia for chemical disarmament:

■ Full and accurate disclosure by Russia of the size of its existing CW stockpile;

■ Demonstrated annual commitment by Russia to allocate at least $25 million to CW elimination;

■ Development by Russia of a practical plan for destroying its stockpile of nerve agents;

■ Enactment of a law, by Russia, that provides for using only a single facility to eliminate all nerve agents; and

■ Agreement by Russia to destroy its chemical production facilities at Volgograd and Novocheboksarsk.[159]

In 2001, when it approved the U.S. federal budget for FY 2002, Congress added one more point to this list: it mandated that for U.S. funding to continue, other members of the international community should demonstrate a commitment to assist in funding and building the infrastructure needed to support and operate the CW elimination facilities.[160]

As a result of the Congress's action, Russia intensified its efforts in chemical disarmament. In turn, the U.S. FY 2002 budget provides for an allocation to Russia of $50 million for these purposes, provided the above conditions are met. Sergei Kirienko, the chairman of the State Commission for Chemical Disarmament, stressed:

> We have succeeded in finding a political solution to the problem. …A year ago, the Americans put forward as conditions for the resumption of assistance a list of requirements that seemed impossible to meet. …However, Russia undertook the task and has met them all. …As far back as last autumn, the U.S. Congress approved the allocation of $50 million for the current year. We have a lot to do ahead of us before we get this money. The main thing that concerns the Americans—has Russia declared everything in its chemical weapons stockpile.[161]

Conditions put on the table by the U.S. Congress are a good illustration of the concerns of the donor countries regarding Russian assistance programs as a whole:

■ Russia can allocate significantly more of its own funds in the elimination of surplus WMD and the facilities for their production;

■ Information supplied by Russia concerning its stockpiles of these weapons and their production capabilities must be reliable;

---

158. Alexander Kalyadin, "The Problem of Timely Dismantlement of the Chemical Weapons Arsenal of the former Soviet Union," *Yaderny Kontrol* (in Russian) No. 2 (March–April 2001).

159. *National Defense Authorization Act for FY 2001*, Public Law 106-398, Sec. 1309.

160. *National Defense Authorization Act for FY 2002*, Public Law 107-107. Sec. 1309.

161. Marina Kalashnikova, "Cooperation Costs More Than Money: Interview with Sergei Kirienko," *Nezavisimaya Gazeta*, February 2, 2002. Kirienko mentioned the possibility of using $80 million from other assistance programs to Russia for chemical disarmament purposes.

■ Decisionmaking in Russia regarding these issues, including the lack of a super-agency to coordinate and implement state-level decisions, is troubling; and

■ The financial and technical details of programs and plans—especially in the medium term—are lacking in Russia.

The Russians, in turn, express discontent that a significant share of the financing does not go to Russia but to foreign enterprises manufacturing the equipment or performing other work associated with the disposition of Russia's surplus military equipment. In addition, Russians are concerned about insufficient coordination of plans and programs, especially among the donor countries, as well as the need for annual approval of appropriations. Some Russian experts believe that the requirement for annual approval hinders the formulation and implementation of long-term programs.

CHAPTER 5

Export Controls

The economic crisis, the liberalization of external economic activities, and the necessity for Russia to be integrated into the world economy have created opportunities for sensitive technologies and information to leak out of Russia. To help prevent such leaks, it has been necessary to create a new Russian export control system and improve customs and border guard services:

- Create a regulatory and legislative base;

- Create an institutional system capable of ensuring that the export control regulations are met;

- Equip border checkpoints and customs houses with the necessary technical equipment; and

- Educate personnel in industrial enterprises, external economic organizations, and government agencies about export control standards and regulations.

Russia has been able to use the experience of developed democratic states in the progress of its export control legislation. Foreign assistance in export control, mainly from the United States, is being carried out in three areas:

- Consultation on legislative, procedural, technical, and other issues associated with the development and performance of the export control system;

- Providing customs houses and border checkpoints (the "second line of defense") with equipment capable of detecting radioactive materials; and

- Training of export control staff.

The comparatively low need for equipment combined with the low—compared with other CTR programs—cost for workshops and other educational and consulting services make for a rather low overall cost for an international assistance program to create an efficient export control system in Russia. In accordance with the 1991 Nunn-Lugar legislation, from 1992 to 1996, 3 percent of all CTR program funds were allocated for assistance in the area of export controls.[162] The funds actually allocated for export control programs went beyond this percentage and amounted to several tens of millions of dollars.

---

162. Zachary Selden, "Nunn-Lugar: New Solutions for Today's Nuclear Threats," BENS Special Report (Washington, D.C.: Business Executives for National Security, September 1997), 8, www.bens.org/pubs_0997.html#top.

Russian Participation in International Export Control Regimes

The formation and functioning of the Russian export control system is linked with Russia's adoption of international agreements and regimes limiting the export of military-purpose products and related items.

According to the Nuclear Non-Proliferation Treaty (NPT), the CWC, and the BWC, Russia shall not transfer nuclear, chemical, or biological weapons to anyone and shall not assist, encourage, or motivate any state to produce or acquire such weapons in any other way. The letter and the spirit of these commitments denote the legally binding prohibition of transfer of raw materials, materials, equipment, technologies, and information that can facilitate the proliferation of WMD.

Russia participates in four—the Wassenaar Arrangements, the Nuclear Suppliers Group, the Zangger Committee, and the Missile Technology Control Regime (MTCR)—out of five multilateral regimes of export control. Russia is not a member of the Australia Group although its commitments under the CWC overlap with the Australia Group's procedures. Commitments under the multilateral regimes are political ones; that fact somewhat reduces their significance and contribution to nonproliferation.

The Russian Export Control System

The inception of Russia's export control system can be dated to 1992, when President Boris Yeltsin signed decree no. 388, "On Measures to Establish an Export Control System in Russia," on June 11, 1992. During the 1990s, Russia established the Interagency Commission on Export Controls; compiled and approved lists of raw materials, finished materials, equipment, scientific and technical information, work, services, and intellectual activities subject to control during export operations; and adopted guidelines regulating external economic activities concerning controlled items.[163]

Normative Basis

The adoption in 1996 of the criminal code of the Russian Federation became one of the key moments in the advancement of the Russian export control system. The code establishes liability for breaching the export control rules. Article 189 is especially devoted to the illegal export of technologies, scientific and technical information and services, raw materials, finished materials and equipment usable

---

163. In the first half of the 1990s Russia introduced the law of the Russian Federation on governmental regulations for foreign trade (adopted in 1995); presidential decree no. 1008 on Russia's military-technical cooperation with foreign states (February 1995); governmental resolution no. 479 on the right of Russian businesses to engage in military-technical cooperation with foreign states (May 1994); and governmental resolution no. 879 on measures for improving the export and import control of military commodities, services, and products resulting from intellectual activities (September 1994).

for the development of WMD, armaments, and military hardware subject to special export controls. Article 189 stipulates that the illegal export of such products is punishable by a hefty fine or a prison sentence of 3–7 years.

Also a number of criminal code articles are closely related to export control: Article 188 on smuggling, Article 220 on the illicit use of nuclear and fissile materials, Article 283 on the divulgence of state secrets, and Article 355 on the production and proliferation of WMD. Violation of export control rules will result in a fine or a prison sentence of up to 10 years in special cases.

The unified system of export control was formalized by the Law on Export Control that was adopted in 1999. The law defined the goods and technologies subject to control. They include raw materials, finished materials, equipment, scientific and technical information, work, services, and the results of intellectual activity that may significantly contribute to creation of WMD, their means of delivery, other armaments, and military hardware.[164]

It is also important that such items include not only goods and technologies especially intended for creation of WMD, the means of their delivery, and other military purposes but also those that exhibit dual-use characteristics. The presence in Russian legislation of two definitions for controlled items—they are goods and technologies that (1) "are usable" in the creation of WMD and that (2) "may significantly contribute" to the creation of WMD—creates difficulties in practical application of the law. The definition of "are usable" is much broader than "may significantly contribute." There is no definition of what is meant by a significant contribution.

The Law on Export Control defines fundamentals of export control in Russia:

■ Discharges obligations included in international agreements to which Russia is a party;

■ Determines principles of state policy;

■ Provides methods of export control, including approval procedures for external economic operations with controlled goods and technologies; and

■ Defines jurisdiction of the state agencies in this field and other key components of the export control system.

The 1999 Law on Export Control serves as the basis for developing guidelines and procedures that are introduced by presidential and governmental decrees, and it constitutes the legal foundation of the Russian export control system. A number of decrees issued by the president and the government establish the jurisdiction of the executive bodies in this area: one example is presidential decree no. 867, "On the Structure of the Federal Executive Agencies," which was adopted in 2000. It created the Ministry of Economic Development and Trade (MEDT) and transferred the main authority for export controls to this ministry.

---

164. *Law on Export Control,* Article 1, Russian Federation.

The Institutional Mechanism

Since 2000, the main export control authority in Russia has been the MEDT. To manage these export control responsibilities, a separate department—the Department of Export Control (DEK)—was created within the MEDT to deal solely with export control. Only the DEK is authorized to grant export licenses for controlled commodities. Besides issuing licenses, the MEDT has two other export control functions: the organization and implementation of an interagency review process (federal expertise) for controlled commodities, technologies, and services; and the accreditation of internal compliance programs (ICPs) adopted by enterprises.

MINATOM, the Ministry of Defense, the Ministry of Foreign Affairs, Gosatomnadzor, the State Customs Committee (GTK), and special services all take part in the interagency federal expertise review. The MEDT must report to MINATOM and the Ministry of Defense on a quarterly basis all information on approved nuclear export licenses. GTK must report to the MEDT on a quarterly basis all information on transfers of controlled items across Russian borders.

There is no formal blacklist of importing states (except for the list of countries that are under UN official sanctions), but during the federal expertise process the Russian Ministry of Foreign Affairs takes into account political considerations such as Russia's participation in international regimes, regime membership of the importing country, Russian bilateral relations, and interests of state.

The GTK verifies the license documents and examines Russian exports to see if they are as listed in the license documents. The GTK also has the right, in certain situations, to delay or halt the exports. The Federal Security Service (FSB) and other agencies may recommend a suspension or halt of export operations for export violations.

The Federal Agency for the Protection of State Intellectual Property (FAPRID) is notified of the intent to export, in conjunction with the license application process, and may recommend the suspension of an exporter's foreign economic activities if it decides state intellectual property rights are being violated.

Other federal institutions such as Rosaviakosmos (the Russian Space Agency), the Russian shipbuilding agency, and the Ministry of Education participate in the system by providing technical reviews of commodities, technologies, or reports under their jurisdiction, and by participating in interagency licensing reviews.

Control Lists

Since the early 1990s Russia has had six control lists that are closely tied to the international regime norms:

■ Nuclear material, components, special nonnuclear material, and technologies;

■ Dual-use equipment, materials, and technologies used in nuclear activities;

■ Dual-use commodities and technologies that are subject to control;

■ Pathogens, genetic material or genetic fragments, genetically altered pathogens, toxins, equipment, and technologies that are subject to control;

■ Chemicals, equipment, and technologies that are dual-use; and

- Equipment, materials, and technologies with missile applications.

These control lists include not only the entry names but also the exact technical specifications of the controlled items, or the range of specifications that render the item in question as controlled. The relevant measures also cover information and results of intellectual activity related to WMD and are aimed at preventing the intangible transfer of technology, which includes education, consultations, and scientific presentations.

MEDT maintains the content of all control lists although several other agencies such as the Ministry of Defense and MINATOM provide input. Changes or additions to these lists require approval by a presidential decree based on a government resolution.

Catchall Control Principle

Of key importance is the Law on Export Control, Article 20, which eliminates any gaps in control lists. It was introduced by the Russian government in 1998 in response to U.S. efforts to ensure effective control with regard to Iran and Iraq. This catchall provides that:

- Russian individuals are prohibited from any participation in external economic activities involving commodities and technologies if they are "confidently aware" that the goods and technologies will be used by "a foreign state or foreign individual" for the purposes of creating WMD and their delivery means;

- Russian participants in external economic activities shall obtain permission for conducting activities with commodities and technologies that are not subject to controlled-item lists if:

  - They have been informed by an authorized federal executive agency in the area of export control that such commodities and technologies can be used for creation of WMD and the means of their delivery, and

  - They have a valid reason to believe that these commodities and technologies may be used for the above purposes.

In addition, the Law on Export Control, Article 18, requires a foreign importer of Russian goods to provide a written statement that the commodities and technologies that are being imported will not be used for creation of WMD or their means of delivery. If the importer intends to import items that Russia prohibits for export, however, the importer most likely will try to conceal it. Exporting organizations in Russia need to have relevant information that allows them to confidently evaluate foreign importers with whom they are trading.

In May 1998, MEDT disseminated two lists to assist exporters. The first was sent to the military's industrial enterprises; it contained a list of end users whose transactions must be approved by competent authorities if they are the recipients of any items, not only sensitive technologies. The second list—prepared by the FSB—was sent to government agencies involved in export control. It listed foreign companies associated with military programs for the creation of WMD and their means of delivery.[165]

The Russian catchall legislation has a substantial drawback. It is extremely difficult for government agencies to prove that a Russian exporter "was confidently aware" or "had a valid reason to believe" that exported items might be used for WMD or WMD delivery systems.

Licenses and the Export Process

Export licenses in Russia are of two types: general and individual. Individual licenses are granted for a single export transaction; general licenses allow the enterprise multiple exports of a certain commodity. General licenses specify only the quantity, not the buyer or end user.[166] General licenses for dual-use items are a recent addition to the export control system, and they require much more scrutiny. The prerequisite for a general license is that the applying enterprise must have a government-certified ICP. General licenses also require a government resolution. Enterprises with a general license must submit quarterly reports to MEDT on the use of the licenses and send copies of these reports to MINATOM if the exported commodity is nuclear related. General licenses are valid for a maximum of 12 months.

The review process for export licenses requires several steps at several decision-making levels: an internal review, a ministerial review, and an interagency review. The internal review, performed by the enterprise itself through its ICP, is the first step. An ICP is defined by the Law on Export Control as a set of organizational, administrative, informational, and other measures followed by the organization's assurance of compliance with export control regulations. ICPs must have MEDT accreditation. In addition to being mandatory for all companies in the military-industrial complex, all MINATOM enterprises, and companies that regularly receive income from foreign companies involved with controlled goods and technologies, ICPs are advantageous for enterprises because they can prevent fines caused by improper export procedures. ICPs are especially effective because they are customized for the nature, size, structure, and exports of each enterprise.

The most important function of the enterprise's ICP is identifying which control list, if any, regulates the export of the product. This is done by noting the product's physical and technical specifications and all possible uses, and then consulting the control lists to see if the specifications make the item a controlled or dual-use item. By Russian law, the responsibility for classification, end-user review, and proper exporting procedure is on the exporter. If a mistake is made in identification, even inadvertently, the enterprise is legally and financially responsible. The internal review must also include a check of the importing company—another legal responsibility of the exporter.

Because most Russian enterprises that export controlled and dual-use commodities are not entirely independent and fall under the total or partial jurisdiction

---

165. Nikolai Uspensky, "Export Controls as a Key Element of National Security," in *Export Control in Russia: Policy and Practices* (in Russian), ed. V. A. Orlov, Report No. 8 (Moscow: PIR Center, 2000), 27–28, www.pircenter.org/english/publications/index.htm.

166. General licenses are permitted only for the export of specific controlled commodities and to specific countries. Lists of such commodities and countries are approved by the government.

of one of the Russian ministries, that ministry performs the next step of the review: determining the financial advisability of permitting the export and the legality of exporting the item. Each ministry has its own system of review, usually involving a specialized review board or committee. Only after a ministry review is a license application sent to MEDT.

The final stage of the review process is performed by the license-issuing authority, MEDT. All license applications are reviewed by MEDT's DEK.[167] At this stage government officials determine whether the export under review has any WMD applications, whether the export would be against Russian economic or national interests, and whether the export would cause Russia to violate any international regimes or agreements to which it is a party.

A license may be denied if:

■ The documents submitted by the applicant contain unreliable, corrupted, or incomplete information;

■ The federal expertise decision is negative; or

■ The external economic transactions with commodities, information, work, services, or the results of intellectual activity are carried out under terms or conditions that damage or pose a threat to the interests of the Russian Federation.

Customs Procedures

Customs is the final stage of the export process. After a license is issued, a cargo declaration must be filed at the regional customs office before export. This declaration includes the export's customs code number (TN VED). When entered into the relevant database, all commodities with a controlled TN VED are red-flagged, alerting customs officials that this export requires a license. At the border, customs officials examine the export license and the customs cargo declaration, verifying that the details listed on both correspond with each other. If they do not, officials may confiscate the shipment and order an investigation. Packages can be physically examined, checked for radioactivity, and even seized. Customs logs all licenses and exports through the Main Research and Computational Center of the GTK.

Customs can stop or even confiscate a shipment of a commodity if it is deemed questionable in any manner. They can examine it, test it for radioactivity, or order a new identification of the commodity if they have doubt about its status on the control list. However, customs will be held financially accountable for the seizure or delay (of more than 10 days) of legitimate exports. Exporters are putting increasing pressure on GTK to expedite exports because they feel the current customs process unnecessarily delays export and hinders profit.

---

167. Mandated under the *Law on Export Control,* Article 21, Official Expert Assessments of Foreign Economic Transactions.

Development of U.S.-Russian Cooperation in Export Controls

U.S.-Russian Cooperation in the 1990s

To receive aid for the creation of a modern export control system, a stand-alone agreement between the United States and Russia concerning cooperation to improve the Russian export control system was drafted in 1993.[168] It was not signed at that time, however, because Russian agencies were very cautious about having the U.S. Department of State as a partner, and they objected to the U.S. requirement to conduct audits of how the assistance was used.

Instead, in January 1994 Russia and the United States signed a memorandum of intent that laid the legal foundation for cooperation in export control and outlined six objectives:

■ Carrying out bilateral and multilateral discussions—at both the political and technical levels—for improving the Russian export control system;

■ Carrying out bilateral discussions on individual multilateral export control regimes and on the technical parameters of the items to be controlled;

■ Training export control system personnel;

■ Facilitating the creation of in-house export control programs encouraging the Russian organizations possessing or producing controlled items to cooperate with the government;

■ Establishing peer review and assistance for improving policies and compliance programs; and

■ Providing the means for tracing controlled items and technologies from the point of origin through the shipping process to the end destination.

Russia's unreadiness to sign the 1993 agreement with the United States led to a long delay in practical cooperation in export control. In April 1995, an informal agreement was achieved to limit the program, in its first stage, to five reciprocal visits by U.S. and Russian experts.

Under the CTR program, from July 1996 through December 1997, 15 cooperative exchanges were conducted between the customs services of Russia and the United States. U.S. funding for export control programs for FY 1997 and beyond was transferred to the Department of State and Department of Energy. As of mid-2002, Russia has not actually been participating in the export control programs undertaken by the U.S. DOD, FBI, and the U.S. Customs Service, which finance equipment; law enforcement; and training of enforcement personnel, customs officers, and frontier guards.[169] U.S. assistance is provided mainly to East European countries and several of the newly independent states.[170]

---

168. The United States had already concluded such export control agreements with Ukraine and Kazakhstan.

169. DOD/FBI Counterproliferation Program and DOD/U.S. Customs Service Counterproliferation Program.

In 1996, the U.S. government transferred the main responsibilities for export control assistance for Russia to the U.S. DOE and the U.S. Department of State. A letter of intent was signed in 1996 concerning cooperation between MINATOM and the DOE; and in 1998 a protocol was signed between DOE and Russia's GTK.

In September 1998, the decision was made to expand cooperation on export control and set up working groups in seven major areas: dual-use technologies, MTCR, nuclear weapons and materials, licensing, ICPs, law enforcement, and customs. After the 2000 elections in the United States, these bilateral working groups ceased their activities. However, the George W. Bush administration has recently made export control a priority area in U.S.-Russia relations. The FY 2003 U.S. budget request for export control programs with Russia has grown substantially— DOE's budget will grow by about 80 percent and the State Departments's budget will double compared with 2002.

Current U.S. Assistance Efforts

Like other U.S. CTR programs, the U.S. export control assistance program is a broad umbrella mechanism that comprises programs in several different agencies. Currently, three U.S. agencies are most actively involved in export control assistance to Russia: DOE's National Nuclear Security Administration (NNSA), the Department of Commerce's Bureau of Industry and Security (BIS, the former Bureau of Export Administration), and the Department of State.[171]

The Department of State works to provide technological and material support to carry out export control assistance as part of its broader nonproliferation efforts. This includes establishing a sufficient legal foundation, providing training and equipment in WMD detection and interdiction, strengthening licensing procedures, helping to install ICPs in exporting enterprises of special concern, and developing and installing software and systems networks for export control information and databases (such as their TRACKER program).

The Department of State also promotes discussion on export controls through bilateral meetings, working groups, and conferences; it also provides supplemental funding for the Commerce Department's BIS and DOE's NNSA activities through its Nonproliferation, Anti-Terrorism, Demining, and Related Programs (NADR) fund. This fund was created in 1999 to expand the possibilities for cooperation with Russia and other former Soviet countries in the area of nonproliferation, including export control.

In 1994, under the Freedom Support Act (FSA) of 1992, the U.S. Department of State created the Nonproliferation and Disarmament Fund (NDF) as a unit of its Disarmament Bureau. During FY 1994–FY 1996, half of its budget was spent on export control activities (table 5.1).

---

170. Scott Parrish and Tamara Robinson, "Efforts to Strengthen Export Controls and Combat Illicit Trafficking and Brain Drain," *Nonproliferation Review* 7, no. 1 (Spring 2000): 116, www.cns.miis.edu/pubs/npr/vol07/71/parish71.pdf.

171. Although the U.S. Customs Service participates in various meetings and discussions on Russian export control issues, no active assistance programs are currently under way.

Table 5.1. Funding for Nonproliferation and Disarmament Fund, FY 1994–FY 2000, millions of U.S. dollars, at current prices

1994	1995	1996	1997	1998	1999	2000
10	10	20	15	15	15	15

Sources: "Nonproliferation, Anti-terrorism, Demining, and Related Programs (NADR),"
www.fas.org/asmp/profiles/aid/fy2001_nadr.htm; www.ndf.org.

Because funding intended for individual countries may change during the course of a year, it is difficult to find the amount of assistance given to Russia only (table 5.2). The U.S. Department of State reports that during FY 1998–FY 2001 the total amount of assistance it rendered for improving Russian export control was $12 million; $5 million was allocated for FY 2002[172] and $10 million was requested for FY 2003.

DOE's export control cooperation with Russia, mainly through the NNSA, began in 1996 when the NNSA's Office of Export Control Policy and Cooperation and MINATOM signed a letter of intent highlighting four goals of cooperation:

■ Scientific analysis of international export control regimes;

■ Export control training at MINATOM enterprises;

■ Seminars and conferences focused on discussions among specialists with export control expertise; and

■ ICP development at MINATOM enterprises.

NNSA currently has identified four major goals in its International Nuclear Export Control Program country plan for Russia and is actively pursuing two of them: promoting industry compliance and strengthening licensing procedures. Since 1996, NNSA has been focusing on industry outreach by holding national, regional, and site-specific workshops. The site-specific workshops—custom-tailored to the individual enterprise—are a new phase for NNSA's Russia program. They help raise awareness of export controls (and why they are necessary), clarify national and international export controls and Russian licensing procedures, and provide a forum for dialogue.

These workshops also educate Russian exporters about their legal export control responsibilities and strengthen the skills necessary to perform a technical review of commodities and thus properly identify commodities.

---

172. The U.S. Department of State, in its report on the implementation of FY 2000 programs, reports that in FY 2000 it spent $7,325,000 for Russian export control assistance programs and $19,680,000 for the corresponding programs in 11 other states—all former Soviet republics. See *FY 2000 Program Performance Report* (Washington, D.C.: U.S. Department of State, April 3, 2001), www.state.gov/m/rm/rls/perfrpt/2000/1902.htm. The report indicates that this amount was earmarked for the improvement of the export control system as well as for programs associated with customs activities. The lack of differentiation between the two purposes complicates the analysis of the amounts of assistance.

Table 5.2. Funding of U.S. Department of State Export Control Programs, FY 2001–FY 2003, millions of U.S. dollars, at current prices

Programs	FY 2001		FY 2002[a]		FY 2003[b]	
	Total	Russia	Total	Russia	Total	Russia
Export Control & Border Security (NADR funds)	19.1	1.5	17.0	1.5	36.0	5.0
Export Control & Border Security (FSA funds)	21.0	3.5	21.0	3.5	40.0	10.0

Source: Kenneth N. Luongo, "Options for Increased U.S.-Russian Nuclear Nonproliferation Cooperation and Projected Costs" (Washington, D.C., RANSAC, October 2001), www.ransac.org/new-web-site/pub/reports/options_paper_101101.html.

a. Estimated.

b. Requested.

The other two goals—working with the GTK to strengthen enforcement and fostering a self-sufficient Russian export control system[173] that functions effectively and independently of U.S. assistance—are more long term. The Office of Export Control and Policy currently is constructing a plan for GTK assistance in training GTK officials and providing them with the informational and technical tools they need to stop illicit exports from Russia.

In FY 2001, DOE financing for assistance programs in the area of export control in Russia and NIS countries was $1.8 million; in FY 2002, $1.9 million. For FY 2003, $3.4 million was requested.[174]

The BIS in the Department of Commerce plays a key part in the coordination of interdepartmental programs associated with export control, visit exchanges, educational workshops, and other similar activities. To attain a healthy export control system, BIS has identified five major goals, or five functional areas, that fall within their assistance capabilities and goals:

■ Program administration and system automation;

■ Legal foundation and regulatory development;

■ Licensing procedures and practices;

■ Export control enforcement mechanisms; and

■ Industry–government relations.

173. Although Russian self-sufficiency is still years away, U.S. assistance programs have made progress in creating a community of technical and academic export control experts. For example, at NNSA workshops Russian technical experts now make a majority of the presentations, and a new generation of technical experts is being pulled into the academic and technical communities.

174. William Hoehn, "Analysis of the Bush Administration's Fiscal Year 2003 Budget Requests for U.S.-Former Soviet Union Nonproliferation Programs" (Washington, D.C.: RANSAC, April 2002), www.ransac.org/new-web-site/related/congress/status/fy2003doe_0402.html.

BIS holds 10 workshops a year on these subjects throughout Russia, and it also develops and distributes related software.

Second Line of Defense

The so-called second line of defense (SLD) is an important element of Russian cooperation in the field of export control. The U.S. DOE and the Russian GTK share responsibility for this element, which is based on the protocol of June 18, 1998, signed by DOE and GTK. In FY 1998 and FY 1999, the United States allocated $3 million annually for this program; in FY 2001 the amount of assistance dropped down to $2.4 million; however, in FY 2002 DOE increased its request for the program to $4 million.[175]

The protocol of June 1998 identified the following areas of cooperation:

■ Improvement of the existing systems and equipment for the detection of nuclear materials;

■ Deployment of nuclear material detection equipment at the border control posts and incorporation of the equipment in the system;

■ Improvement in the training of personnel in detection and identification of nuclear materials and associated dual-use commodities, accomplished through the education of customs personnel, development of training programs, and supplying needed equipment; and

■ Improvement in the detection of nuclear materials and improved identification techniques.

GTK order no. 241 of May 7, 1997, identified 18 customs houses authorized to receive customs declarations on the export and import of fissile and radioactive materials. The customs facilities were furnished with equipment to determine the isotopic composition of incoming and outgoing material in order to prevent the possibility of transporting an undeclared shipment. Russia has developed the radioactive-material detection system, Yantar, that has been granted a certificate of compliance with U.S. standards for radiation monitors after being tested at the Los Alamos National Laboratory. The version of Yantar designed for use with railroad cars is unique; it is capable of registering the number of a railcar in which radioactive material is present. The railcar- or truck-monitoring system costs $35,000–$40,000; a similar system that monitors individuals costs $14,000.

Under the SLD program, the branches of the Russian Customs Academy were equipped with the necessary radiation-monitoring hardware and office equipment for the training of customs officers in the processing and control of nuclear and radioactive materials.

The amount the United States has appropriated for Russian producers under the SLD program is higher than the United States has appropriated for any other program related to the elimination of the Cold War legacy. It is significant to Russia that the equipment and hardware are being designed and manufactured by domestic producers.

---

175. Ibid.

Russian Export Controls: Achievements and Problems

Russian experts understandably believe that Russia's decision to base its export control system on the Western experience has created a national export control system that meets international standards. Contact with Western partners has helped improve individual elements of the system. The adoption of the Law on Export Control has increased the status of some export control mechanisms that previously functioned on the basis of governmental or presidential decrees and has resulted in a significant amount of work to bring rules and regulations into compliance with the law.

Work is under way to develop and strengthen internal compliance programs. In May 1998, the Russian government published the *Manual for Establishing Internal Compliance Programs at Russian Enterprises.* Enterprises were expected to appoint an official responsible for export control issues. This official would report directly to the enterprise manager and would have broad authority, including the right to suspend export operations and to act if circumstances might lead to a breach of Russian legislation or the failure by Russia to fulfill its international commitments.

The state is attempting to expand control over all channels open for the international transfer of technology and is paying special attention to the so-called intangible forms of technology transfer, including personal contacts (scientific conferences, meetings, discussions, scientific exchanges, presentations, inspections, consultations, demonstrations, technical assistance, lectures, seminars, and education including training of foreign students) and communication via e-mail, facsimile, and telephone. The regulatory documents stipulate that the state has control over technical data transfers as well as over the intangible forms of technology transfer. The annexes to the control lists define such terms as technology and technical data, and they indicate what forms of technology transfer are not subject to control. These disclaimers, related to the public domain, have been borrowed to a certain extent from corresponding U.S. legislation. Many problems regarding control over intangible technologies still need to be resolved. The development of a unified approach to this problem, including unified law enforcement, will require efforts as serious as those needed to strengthen international cooperation.

In a positive shift, Russian federal agencies responsible for export control have recently started to pay more attention to education in export control. For example, at the regular MINATOM-DOE scientific and practical conferences and workshops for the enterprises under their jurisdiction, experts have noted a significant increase in the qualifications and knowledge of the theory and practices of export control of the enterprise specialists responsible for applying for licenses. Polls of workshop participants also confirm this.

Export control efficiency still needs improvement: interaction between the state and the industrial community needs to be strengthened, and trust between parties needs to be improved. In particular, the exporter must clearly understand why the state imposes certain constraints on foreign economic activities. This will make interaction between industry and the state more efficient. At the same time, Russian federal authorities still disseminate very little material on export control issues—

including legislation and regulations. As a result, it is difficult for the exporters to keep track of all the legal and administrative changes regarding export control.

Russia, as other countries, faces practical difficulties in implementing the catch-all control article of the Law on Export Control. Russian experts are interested in the legal nuances of the relevant legislation in different countries and to what extent it is feasible to implement them in Russia.

Large tasks still remain: installing the necessary equipment at all customs houses and broadening the customs staff's knowledge of export control law. Ongoing programs are directed at finding sustainable funding for already existing projects instead of creating entirely new projects.

Russia's export control programs have been recognized thus far in the United States as effective in their goals. However, the Russian export control system is far from mature, and more work is needed. The National Export Control Evaluation Project, under the auspices of the University of Georgia's Center for International Trade and Security (CITS), recently analyzed the national export control systems of more than 20 nations, assigning them scores on various elements of their export control systems for a maximum possible score of 100. Russia received a score of 76.29, placing it significantly below Ukraine, the United Kingdom, Japan, and the United States, and approximately equal to China, South Korea, India, and Cuba.[176] BIS's 2002 foreign policy report places the Russian export control system for high-performance computers in the third tier of nations that includes Israel, Kazakhstan, Tajikistan, and Uzbekistan—countries widely regarded as having less proliferation-proof export control systems.[177]

The CITS evaluation assigned scores for 10 elements of national export control systems. Russia scored relatively high in such categories as licensing, control lists, and international regime membership. However, it scored poorly on customs, verification, and penalties.

In sum, the following work is needed:

■ Borders. Customs is the very last line of defense in terms of export controls. The Russian border is more than 61,000 km long (as an example, Russia shares a 7,500 km open border with Kazakhstan).[178] Effective protection in such conditions would be difficult even if the Russian customs service could be furnished with all necessary equipment and its personnel perfectly trained in export control. Although the customs service has been responsible for export control since 1995, it is still too poorly equipped to be efficient in controlling the Russian borders.

---

176. "Cross National Comparison of Export Control Systems (10 Elements, 100 Point Scale)," table 1 (Athens, Ga.: Center for International Trade and Security, University of Georgia, n.d.), www.uga.edu/cits/ttxc/nat_eval_nec_table.htm.

177. "Computer Tier Country Chart," BXA Foreign Policy Report to Congress (Washington, D.C.: Bureau of Science and Industry, U.S. Department of Commerce, January 18, 2002), Appendix 3, www.bxa.doc.gov/press/2002/ForeignPolicyReport02/Appendi3_ComputerTierChart.pdf.

178. Michael Beck, Marina Katsva, and Igor Khripunov, "Assessing Proliferation Controls in Russia" (Athens, Ga.: Center for International Trade and Security, University of Georgia, n.d.), http://www.uga.edu/cits/ttxc/nat_eval_Russia_2001.htm.

- Personnel. Customs officers also often lack the knowledge and experience to detect and identify commodities subject to control and to use effectively the methodological guides for identification of export items and the equipment available to them. In spite of the continued strengthening of GTK hardware capabilities, many of the customs houses are still poorly equipped. Also, customs officers are still low-paid government employees, a fact that encourages corruption.

- Verification. As many foreign experts believe, Russia is unable to verify how the transferred items are to be used.

- Liability. Russian legislation imposes on individuals found guilty of infractions only a small financial liability for violation of export regulations. Because the financial penalties are negligible compared with the revenues from the sale of controlled commodities, the current penalties cannot be an efficient deterrent.

These weaknesses of the Russian export control system identify areas where improvements must be made and international assistance could be put to good use:

- Assisting industrial enterprises and external trade organizations in creating internal compliance programs and in training of personnel;

- Furnishing necessary equipment to customs houses as well as basic and advanced training for customs house personnel—especially in skills and methods needed for identifying controlled items and in the use of databases;

- Expanding access to information about importers that pose a threat in terms of proliferation of WMD and the means of their delivery; and

- Identifying enterprises and organizations with the highest proliferation risk.

U.S.-Russia and multilateral cooperation in the field of export control could be enhanced if the countries could reach an agreement on which countries are limited or prohibited from receiving controlled items. This would remove many problems and disagreements at the political level that poison U.S.-Russia relations and impede external assistance in the area of export control.

CHAPTER 6

Downsizing and Conversion of Russia's Nuclear Weapons Complex

After the breakup of the Soviet Union, many former Soviet military-industrial and military-scientific establishments faced desperate socioeconomic conditions, aggravated by the fact that a substantial number of military facilities and scientific centers were subject to downsizing, conversion, restructuring, or closing. As a result, it became widely feared that these facilities, design offices, and institutes would become sources for the proliferation of information regarding the design, manufacture, and delivery of WMD.

It is difficult to estimate the validity of such fears, as well as the scale of danger, that could be caused by the leakage of sensitive information and technology. The wholesale acquisition of foreign technology and information could substantially shorten the time and reduce the costs needed to develop new weapons. For example, in Germany in 1945, the Soviet Union and the United States seized many documents related to missile construction, missile equipment, finished missiles, and missile components as well as several hundred rocket scientists. This seizure significantly reduced the time required to begin the manufacturing of missiles in the United States and the Soviet Union. Information provided by Soviet intelligence services working in the United States and Great Britain greatly reduced the time needed for the development of Soviet nuclear weapons. Other examples are similar: advancements in Chinese nuclear missile potential and development of the North Korean ballistic missile program. North Korean ballistic missiles were modeled after the Soviet missile, Scud-B, obtained from Egypt (in turn, the Scud-B is a modern version of the German missile V2). All the cases mentioned involved the systematic collection of vast amounts of information, or the work of large teams of foreign scientists, or the obtaining of equipment and technologies that allowed these countries to begin the production of weapons.

The experience of the 1990s shows that there were no substantial illicit leakages of sensitive information and technologies from the states of the former Soviet Union; at least, there is no convincing evidence of that occurring. But there have been known attempts by states of concern to obtain in Russia some sort of information and technology related to their programs for WMD and their means of delivery. It is probable that such attempts will continue. The success of those attempts will facilitate greatly the development of military programs in those rogue states. International efforts that are focused on the reduction of socioeconomic difficulties in the former Soviet military-industrial and military-scientific establishments should help prevent the success of such attempts. Efforts should first be focused on civilian employment of former military experts.

Scale of the Problem

The Russian nuclear weapons complex (NWC) enterprises are mainly concentrated in the closed administrative-territorial formations (CATFs) of the MINATOM system, which supported a population of about 760,000 in 2000.[179] Only a small percentage of these residents actually work at the NWC enterprises, but because those enterprises support their satellite cities, life in the CATFs depends greatly on the situation within the NWCs.

The total number of specialists who work on government-mandated defense projects in the NWCs is about 75,000,[180] including employees of NWC facilities situated outside of MINATOM's CATFs.[181] Western sources estimate that 2,000 to 4,000 of the specialists possess critically important information on nuclear weapons and nuclear weapons manufacture. An additional 10,000 to 15,000 specialists are able to carry out important auxiliary duties.[182] These estimates are substantially lower than the widely believed assumptions that there are tens of thousands of experts who are able to render technical assistance to the military nuclear programs of rogue states.

The reduction of military nuclear programs is under way. On April 11, 2001, Lev Ryabev, the first deputy minister of MINATOM, stated, "By 2003 there will be two nuclear warhead assembly and dismantlement plants instead of four, and one plutonium and uranium components fabrication plant instead of two," and "the total number of specialists who work on government-mandated defense projects in the nuclear weapons complex will be reduced from 75,000[183] to 35,000–40,000 within five to seven years."[184] The CATFs that support large nuclear-fuel-cycle enterprises whose capabilities may be easily directed toward civilian-commercial activities have found themselves less affected by the crisis. The centers for the assembly and dismantlement of nuclear warheads, where the opportunity to

---

179. Oleg Bukharin, Frank von Hippel, and Sharon K. Weiner, *Conversion and Job Creation in Russia's Closed Nuclear Cities: An Update, Based on a Workshop Held in Obninsk, Russia, June 27–29, 2000* (Princeton: Program on Nuclear Policy Alternatives of the Center for International Studies of the Center for Energy and Environmental Studies, Princeton University, November 2000), 13, www.princeton.edu/~globsec/publications/pdf/obninsk1.pdf.

180. Lev Ryabev, first deputy minister of atomic energy (report to the Russian Federation State Duma, April 11, 2001), www.ransac.org/new-web-site/pub/nuclearnews/04.13.01.html.

181. Vladimir Bocharov, head of division, Institute for Strategic Stability, MINATOM (comments during a roundtable discussion, PIR Center, Moscow, March 27, 2002).

182. Sokolski and Riisager, eds., *Beyond Nunn-Lugar.*

183. "The number 75,000 includes the NWC enterprises beyond CATF boundaries," Vladimir Bocharov, head of division, Institute for Strategic Stability, MINATOM (comments during a roundtable discussion, PIR Center, Moscow, March 27, 2002).

184. Lev Ryabev, first deputy minister of atomic energy (report to the Russian Federation State Duma, April 11, 2001), www.ransac.org/new-web-site/pub/nuclearnews/04.13.01.html.

Table 6.1. Specialization of MINATOM CATFs

CATF	Specialty
Sarov (Arzamas-16)	Development and scientific support of nuclear weapons; serial production and dismantling of nuclear warheads
Snezhinsk (Chelyabisk-70)	Development and scientific support of nuclear weapons
Lesnoi (Sverdlovsk-45)	Serial production and dismantling of nuclear warheads
Zarechnyi (Penza-19)	Serial production and dismantling of nuclear warheads
Trekhgorhyi (Zlatoust-36)	Serial production and dismantling of nuclear warheads
Ozersk (Chelyabinsk-65)	Complex of nuclear-fuel-cycle enterprises
Seversk (Tomsk-7)	Complex of nuclear-fuel-cycle enterprises
Zheleznogorsk (Krasnoyarsk-26)	Complex of nuclear-fuel-cycle enterprises
Zelenogorsk (Krasnoyarsk -45)	Uranium enrichment/downblending plant

Source: Oleg Bukharin, "Post–Cold War Consolidation of Nuclear Weapons Complexes in the United States and in Russia," *Yaderny Kontrol* (in Russian), No. 5 (September–October 1999): 43–56.

develop commercial enterprises is weak, have suffered to a higher degree. The scientific centers are somewhere in between.[185] See table 6.1 for a list of CATFs.

The Russian government has made efforts to create new jobs and refocus the existing jobs in the CATFs, but economic difficulties underscore the importance of international assistance in resolving these problems. Industrial and research facilities are situated in both the CATFs and the big cities. The number of specialists who have access to sensitive information on chemical and biological weapons was estimated to be 5,000 to 10,000.[186] However, the number of experts employed in civilian research who still have some sensitive (biological or chemical) knowledge is much higher than in the nuclear complexes. Therefore, it is crucially important to provide the 7,000 to 12,000 scientists and engineers with adequate employment.

But this is only one part of the problem. The desperate socioeconomic conditions at the military-industrial and military-scientific complexes could compel their employees to steal weapons-grade materials, equipment components, and

---

185. Valentin Tikhonov, *Nuclear-Missile Complex of Russia: Mobility of Personnel and Security,* Working Papers, Issue 1 (in Russian) (Moscow: Carnegie Moscow Center, 2000), http://pubs.carnegie.ru/english/workpapers/default.asp?n=list2000.asp.

186. Sokolski and Riisager, eds., *Beyond Nunn-Lugar.*

technical documents. It is extremely undesirable to let such dangerous materials, equipment, and information fall into the hands of terrorists or rogue states.

Information Leakage

The possibility that WMD-related experts would immigrate to the rogue states is extremely dangerous, but the widely believed estimates regarding the scale of this brain drain are not true. Despite the fact that many experts want to work outside of Russia, only 1 percent have emigrated. They are ignorant of what active and deliberate steps they need to take in order to emigrate, and they are also reluctant to do so. There are also economic difficulties associated with emigrating. Currently, the internal brain drain prevails over the external one.[187] The most popular foreign destinations for emigration are not rogue states; they are European countries, the United States, and Israel. Nevertheless, it is impossible to exclude completely the possibility of WMD-related specialists immigrating to states of concern.

The accessibility of up-to-date electronic communications also raises to dangerous levels the threat of intangible transfers of information. This is just one additional reminder that cooperative job creation and conversion programs, as well as the creative development of satisfactory solutions to the socioeconomic problems in the CATFs, are very important and meet the national security interests of both Russia and the donor states. Donor countries realize the necessity of such assistance. A U.S. General Accounting Office report published in May 2001 states that efforts by the U.S. DOE to create sustainable jobs for the Russian weapons scientists in the commercial sector as well as reduce the Russian nuclear weapons complex undoubtedly serve U.S. security interests.[188]

Programs to Aid Russian Scientists

To prevent the threat that disaffected scientists and experts will facilitate the proliferation of sensitive information about the development of WMD, international programs have been set up, including the Initiatives for Proliferation Prevention (IPP), the Nuclear Cities Initiative (NCI), the International Science and Technology Center (ISTC), the Civilian Research and Development Foundation (CRDF), and the European Nuclear Cities Initiative (ENCI).

---

187. Internal emigration is emigration from a CATF to other locations inside Russia. External emigration is emigration to another country.

188. Gary L. Jones, "Nuclear Nonproliferation: DOE's Efforts To Secure Nuclear Material and Employ Weapons Scientists in Russia," statement before the Subcommittee on Emerging Threats and Capabilities, Committee on Armed Services, U.S. Senate, May 15, 2001, Report No. GAO-01-726T (Washington, D.C.: U.S. General Accounting Office, May 2001), www.gao.gov/new.items/d01726t.pdf.

Table 6.2. Distribution of IPP Funding

State	Percentage received
Russia	84
Ukraine	9
Kazakhstan	4
Belarus	3

Source: "Nuclear Nonproliferation: Concerns with DOE's Efforts to Reduce the Risks Posed by Russia's Unemployed Weapons Scientists," Report No. GAO/RCED-99-54 (Washington, D.C.: U.S. General Accounting Office, February 19, 1999), 21, www.gao.gov/archive/1999/rc99054.pdf.

Table 6.3. Funding Phases of IPP Projects

Phase	Source of funds
Phase 1	Projects are financed by the U.S. government and are focused on laboratory-to-laboratory cooperation and direct contact between Russian and U.S. institutions.
Phase 2	Projects are joined by industrial enterprises, which must invest funds equal to that of the state.
Phase 3	State funding is not involved/required.

Source: "Nuclear Nonproliferation: Concerns with DOE's Efforts to Reduce the Risks Posed by Russia's Unemployed Weapons Scientists," Report No. GAO/RCED-99-54.

Initiatives for Proliferation Prevention

In 1994, the U.S. DOE launched its Industrial Partnering Program, a program that since 1996 has been called the Initiatives for Proliferation Prevention. Program funds are allocated not only for Russia, although it consumes the majority of the funds. Funds also reach Ukraine, Kazakhstan, and Belarus as well (table 6.2). Cooperation is primarily targeted to the reduction of nuclear proliferation threats (70 percent of the projects[189]). Projects related to chemistry and biology are also covered. The IPP program targets several tasks, both short term (the involvement of weapons scientists in civilian projects) and long term (the creation of sustainable jobs for former weapons scientists in the high-tech commercial sector and the involvement of private partners).

Those involved with the IPP program believe that the implemented projects must be commercially beneficial for the United States as well as for partners in the former Soviet Union (see table 6.3). At the same time, however, the main goal is the

189. Wolfsthal et al., *Nuclear Status Report*, 71.

Table 6.4. Funding of IPP Program, FY 1994–FY 2002, millions of U.S. dollars

FY 1994	FY 1995	FY 1996	FY 1997	FY 1998	FY 1999	FY 2000	FY 2001	FY 2002
35.0	0	20.0	29.6	29.6	22.5	24.5	24.1	36.0

Sources: FY 1994 through FY 2000: Wolfsthal et al., *Nuclear Status Report,* 71; FY 2001 and FY 2002: "Defense Nuclear Nonproliferation, Proposed Appropriation Language," www.mbe.doe.gov/budget/03budget/content/defnn/nuclnonp.pdf.

reduction of threats to the nonproliferation regime. One of the main requirements for receiving financing for a particular project is that the majority of participants have knowledge of nuclear, biological, or chemical weapons production.

Implementation of the IPP from 1994 to 2002 yielded the following results:[190]

■ Projects involved 13,000 scientists from countries of the former USSR;

■ More than 850 new high-tech jobs have been created in Russia;

■ 203 projects are currently under way; 64 of these are in the closed nuclear cities in Russia;

■ $90 million in IPP funding has attracted $125 million in private sector matches;

■ Two IPP projects were the basis of R&D 100 awards for the top 100 U.S. technological developments of 2000; and

■ 13 projects have been commercialized—five projects have attracted more than $60 million in venture capital.

In February 1999, the U.S. General Accounting Office published an IPP implementation report.[191] The GAO's most serious criticisms were:

■ Inadequate distribution of allocated funds: only 37 percent was being spent in countries of the former USSR; a substantial amount was being spent for administrative and overhead charges;

■ Lack of steady funding: this had an impact on strategic planning (see table 6.4 for information from additional sources);

■ The very low number of commercially viable projects that were capable of reaching the break-even point: out of more than four hundred projects, only eight succeeded commercially);

■ Insufficient control on the part of the U.S. project managers and a lack of transparency on Russian and NIS side, in particular regarding participants in the projects; and

---

190. Initiatives for Proliferation Prevention, U.S. Department of Energy, http://ipp.lanl.gov/ipp/ippext.nsf/Results?OpenPage.

191. "Nuclear Nonproliferation: Concerns with DOE's Efforts to Reduce the Risks Posed by Russia's Unemployed Weapons Scientists," Report No. GAO/RCED-99-54 (Washington, D.C.: U.S. General Accounting Office, February 19, 1999), www.gao.gov/archive/1999/rc99054.pdf.

Table 6.5. Funding of NCI Program, FY 1999–FY 2002, millions of U.S. dollars

FY 1999	FY 2000	FY 2001	FY 2002
15.0	7.5	27.5	21.0

Sources: FY 1999 through FY 2001: Wolfsthal et al., *Nuclear Status Report,* 71; FY 2002: "Defense Nuclear Nonproliferation, Proposed Appropriation Language," www.mbe.doe.gov/budget/03budget/content/defnn/nuclnonp.pdf.

- Incomplete diversion of NWC specialists from military research to civilian work: many Russian participants employed on IPP projects continued to work on Russian- or NIS-mandated defense projects for part of the time. Thus, the main goal of the initiative has not been achieved.

Nuclear Cities Initiative

The NCI program was started in 1998 after MINATOM and DOE signed an intergovernmental agreement. Funding for this program has fluctuated; see table 6.5. This program has one main goal: the creation of new jobs for specialists who were involved in the development of WMD. Two secondary goals have also been put forward to help eliminate possible threats to the nonproliferation regime:

- Reduce the size of MINATOM's nuclear weapons complex;

- Establish civil-society institutions in the CATFs.

The initial stage of the NCI initiative focused on three closed cities: Sarov, Snezhinsk, and Zheleznogorsk (see table 6.1) and worked toward developing strategic development plans that enhance infrastructure to improve investment attractiveness. The most significant NCI projects included:

- Sarov's computer center, which provided 40 percent of all jobs created under the NCI program;

- Transfer of several buildings from the electro-mechanical plant Avangard in order to set up the production of medical equipment in a joint undertaking with the U.S. company, Fresenius Medical Care;[192] and

- Creation of international business development centers in Snezhinsk and Zheleznogorsk in order to resolve the main problems hindering the business development process in the nuclear cities: a lack of information about external markets, insufficient practical business skills for dealing with free-market conditions, and a lack of capital.

During its two first years, the NCI enjoyed only minor success in creating new jobs—a total of 370 individuals found work. The majority of these people did part-

---

192. "This project seems to be a kind of indicator for the U.S. partners; its successful implementation can open the way for the programs larger in scale," Vladimir Sterekhov, MINATOM employee (comments during roundtable discussions at the PIR Center, Moscow, March 27, 2002).

Table 6.6. Recipients of NCI Program Funding, FY 1999–FY 2000

Source	Share (percent)
U.S. national laboratories	67
U.S. DOE headquarters	3
Russia	30

Source: "Nuclear Nonproliferation: DOE's Efforts to Assist Weapons Scientists in Russia's Nuclear Cities Face Challenges," Report No. GAO-01-429 (Washington, D.C.: U.S. General Accounting Office, May 2001), www.nti.org/db/nisprofs/russia/fulltext/gaorpts/gaonci.pdf.

time work under NCI and continued to work on government-mandated defense projects.[193]

On the whole, the main difficulties faced by the NCI program are the same that are faced by the IPP. About half of the 26 NCI projects involved the development of social infrastructure and civil society in the CATFs (i.e., supplies of medical equipment and school-to-school exchanges). The DOE believes that these projects should have improved the investment climate in the CATFs, but the Russian program participants and industry representatives disagreed strongly because investment attractiveness does not depend on the level of social infrastructure development. In addition, as in the case of IPP, most of the project funds were spent in the United States (see table 6.6) although, following the programmatic logic, they should have been spent in the Russian closed scientific centers.

After FY 2003, the IPP and NCI programs will be merged into the Russian Transition Initiative.

International Science and Technology Center

The ISTC was established in 1992 by the European Union, Russia, the United States, and Japan. Eventually Norway and South Korea joined as donor countries, and Armenia, Belarus, Georgia, Kazakhstan, and the Kyrgyz Republic joined as recipients. In accordance with the ISTC agreement, the center pursues the following objectives:

- Providing opportunities for scientists and specialists involved in the development of weapons to reorient their talents to peaceful activities; those who possess knowledge and skills in the development of WMD and WMD delivery systems are sought as participants; and

- Facilitating through its projects and activities:

  - Resolution of national and international technical problems;

  - Transition (on a broader scale) to a market economy;

---

193. Jones, "Nuclear Nonproliferation: DOE's Efforts To Secure Nuclear Material and Employ Weapons Scientists in Russia," Report No. GAO-01-726T, 3.

Table 6.7. Distribution of Funding to ISTC Scientific Areas, 2002

Scientific areas	Percentage of funding
Biotechnology and life science	23.0
Environment	16.1
Physics	11.8
Fission reactors	11.3
Materials	9.8
Instrumentation	5.4
Chemistry	4.4
Space, aircraft and surface transportation	4.2
Information and communication	3.9
Manufacturing technology	3.6
Nonnuclear energy	2.5
Fusion	2.4
Other	1.6

Source: "ISTC Projects by Technology Area," International Science and Technology Center, www.istc.ru; http://212.44.146.6/cgi%2Dbin/wcscgi.exe/reports/ TechArea.last.rpt?cmd=get_pg&viewer=html_page&vfmt=html_page&page=1&brch=&.

- Support of fundamental and applied research and technical developments primarily in the area of environmental protection, energy generation, and nuclear power safety; and

- Integration of scientists from the Commonwealth of Independent States (CIS) and Georgia into the scientific world community.

To achieve these objectives, the ISTC develops, approves, finances, and monitors scientific and technical projects intended for peaceful applications. These are carried out in research institutes and at facilities located in the Russian Federation as well as in other CIS countries. The main scientific areas being supported through the ISTC projects are fundamental and nuclear physics, ecology (rehabilitation of the environment), and biotechnology (see table 6.7).

ISTC activities are mainly implemented through the Scientific and Technical Projects program and Partnership Support program. In the framework of the Partnership Support program, the ISTC provides financial, organizational, and technical support to projects that are being developed by scientists from the CIS countries and those that are developed with support of international organizations. VNIIEF, VNIITF, Bochvar Institute, IPPE, MEPhI, and others are listed among the institutions that are cooperating most actively with the ISTC.

The Partnership Support program provides private industry, scientific institutes, and other governmental and nongovernmental organizations with the opportunity to finance (through the ISTC) research carried out in the CIS institutes. Cooperation with the ISTC gives the partners a number of advantages:

- Well-developed project management structure of the ISTC; and

Table 6.8. Sources of ISTC Funds, 2002

Source	Funding (percent)
United States	35.6
European Union	26.9
Japan	11.7
South Korea	0.4
Norway	0.4
Partners/other	25.0

Source: "ISTC Projects by Funding Source," International Science and Technology Center, www.istc.ru; http://212.44.146.6/cgi%2Dbin/wcscgi.exe/reports/ByParties.last.rpt?cmd=get_pg&viewer=html_page&vfmt=html_page&page=1&brch=&.

■ Financing as well as imported equipment are exempted from all taxes and duties in accordance with the ISTC agreement.

By 2002, the ISTC partners list included more than 100 large private and public research organizations in the European Union, the United States, Japan, and South Korea. As of March 30, 2002, 1,483 projects were financed through the ISTC for a total of $409 million.[194] Of this amount, 25 percent was allocated by the ISTC partners (table 6.8).

As assessed by a number of experts, the ISTC is the most efficient program for diverting military sector specialists to peaceful research. The ISTC, however, does not require that an individual leave the traditional work organization to get financing (table 6.9). In 2000, the majority of scientists involved in ISTC projects spent less than 25 percent of their work time on them.[195] In addition, the ISTC activities are targeted at scientific and technical community representatives—but not the laborers—who work in the defense industry.

One of the main advantages of the ISTC program may be its many-sided nature, the collectivity of its decisionmaking process, and its well-mastered interaction procedures. Cooperation within the framework of the ISTC is carried out on the basis of a depoliticized laboratory-to-laboratory principle that facilitates the establishment of working relations and leads to the declared goal: diverting to civilian activities the scientists previously involved in military programs. The success of the ISTC is shown by the fact that recently the United States—the key donor to the centers—has been gradually increasing its budgetary allocations to the program (table 6.10).[196]

---

194. ISTC Database Graphs and Tables, International Science and Technology Center, Moscow, Russia, www.istc.ru/istc/website.nsf/fm/z12+Graphs.

195. Annual Report, ISTC, 2000.

196. "FY 2003 International Affairs (Function 150) Budget Request" (Washington, D.C.: Bureau of Resource Management, U.S. Department of State, February 4, 2002), 23, 65 www.state.gov/documents/organization/9194.pdf.

Table 6.9. Time Spent by Russian Scientists on Work under ISTC Grants

Time spent	Number of scientists	Time (percent)
1–25 days	7,715	36.3
26–50 days	4,435	20.8
51–76 days	2,959	13.9
76–100 days	2,372	11.2
101–150 days	1,994	9.4
151–200 days	1,222	5.7
More then 200 days	576	2.7
Total	21,273	100.0

Source: Annual Report, ISTC, 2000.

U.S. Civilian Research and Development Fund

The U.S. Civilian Research and Development Fund (CRDF) also participates in a number of programs targeted to create civilian business opportunities for scientists previously involved in defense programs. The assistance being provided by this fund is mainly linked with ISTC activities and is directed to supporting the assessment of projects submitted for ISTC review and for facilitating contact between scientists from the former Soviet Union and U.S. partners. Its goal is developing projects to be submitted for ISTC review. Between 1998 and 2000, under the grant programs for joint research, the CRDF supported projects worth a total of $11.5 million. One of the fund's stipulations is that not less than 80 percent of the grants allocated for the participants from the former Soviet Union be spent in the former Soviet Union.

European Nuclear Cities Initiative

Under the framework of the European Nuclear Cities Initiative (ENCI), a number of small-sized projects are being created for the cities of Snezhinsk and Sarov. The cities serve as consulting or production entities under stringent coordination or under the leadership of their potential consumers/clientele.[197] ENCI has established an international working group with goals that include:

- Review of past and current activities targeted at resolving problems within the closed cities;

---

197. Paolo Cotta Ramusino, Didier Gambier, Antonino Lantieri, and Maurizio Martellini, "The European Nuclear Cities Initiative (ENCI), the International Working Group and the Debt-for-Security Swap Concept: A View from Italy and the European Commission" (paper presented at Carnegie Non-Proliferation Conference, Washington, D.C., June 18–19, 2001), http://lxmi.mi.infn.it/~landnet/Doc/enci_carnegie.pdf.

Table 6.10. U.S. Funding for Scientific and Technical Centers in Russia and the NIS, FY 2001–FY 2003, millions of U.S. dollars

FY 2001	FY 2002 (est.)	FY 2003 (request)
35.0	37.0	52.0

Source: "FY 2003 International Affairs (Function 150) Budget Request" (Washington, D.C.: Bureau of Resource Management, U.S. Department of State, February 4, 2002), 23, 65, www.state.gov/documents/organization/9194.pdf.

- Review of the measures that would lead to merging the efforts of various programs and projects;

- Identification of potential donors and financial mechanisms to support ENCI efforts associated with the conversion of CATFs and the creation of new jobs in the CATFs.

The Future of Assistance Programs to Redirect the Careers of Russian NWC Scientists

Programs to redirect and retrain NWC scientists in Russia have not yet been successful in solving two important problems. First, the redirection of former WMD specialists to civilian projects has not yet been guaranteed; many work on both the new civilian projects as well as their traditional military projects. Second, the new projects that were created to employ these specialists have not been economically successful. Economic viability of a project is considered to be the key criterion to the project's success.

The business failures of these projects are caused, most likely, by the inability to verify compliance of the proposed projects with the goals of the program, and by a lack of control over the projects' realization. A lack of necessary information (for example, previous involvement of project's participants in military programs) may very well be at the root of the problem.

Donor states are currently revising their approaches to assistance programs for Russia. The major goal of the donor states is still the creation of new employment possibilities for the specialists who formerly worked in the USSR's military-industrial and military-scientific complexes. Recently, however, more attention is being paid to the creation of a stable and long-term dialogue between Russia and the donor states. Above all, the affected parties have begun to realize that preventing leaks of sensitive information requires solving preexisting socioeconomic and cultural problems.

CHAPTER 7

Prospects for International Assistance to Russia

The prospects for international assistance to Russia in eliminating the Cold War legacy depend on both the availability of resources in the donor states and the funds that Russia may independently invest. An important step forward was the agreement reached by the G-8 states to allocate $20 billion over 10 years for these purposes. However, this is far too little to resolve the complete problem. Misunderstandings between Russia and the donor countries, primarily the United States, that have accrued during program implementation must be resolved first. Concerns and dissatisfaction have been raised in Russia as well as in the donor states, and they may impede further development of international cooperation in this important area. It is also necessary to improve the effective use of monies appropriated.

In Russian political circles and federal agencies there exists the widespread belief that national security interests need to prevail over the benefits from international financial assistance rendered to meet treaty commitments related to reducing WMD and ensuring the safety and security of weapons-grade materials. Although such a viewpoint is valid, the question remains: "What falls under these national security interests?" Bilateral efforts to ensure security on the one hand and eliminate the Cold War legacy on the other do not take into account that the threats to Russia's national security are primarily due to international terrorism, the proliferation of WMD and their means of delivery, local conflicts, and instability near the Russian borders. Therefore, with conditions as they are today, the elimination of surplus WMD and secure storage of stockpiles are absolutely necessary for Russia. The protection of weapons materials and technologies and the creation of new jobs for employees of the military-industrial complex currently under reduction both fully correspond with Russia's key security interests.

At the G-8 meeting in June 2002, President Vladimir V. Putin of Russia unambiguously acknowledged the link between the fight against terrorism and the necessity of eliminating surplus stockpiles of WMD:

> The theme of a global fight against terrorism has long been under discussion. It is linked to Russia, to some other countries in which definite arsenals are concentrated, stockpiles of weapons of mass destruction in the first place. To Russia this is a relevant theme since we have inherited several rather complicated problems from the Soviet Union, of which the chief ones are the debt of the former Soviet Union, with which we are coping, for all the problems, as you know, and a large quantity of arms long since inoperative, stored and earmarked for destruction. I mean, first of all, atomic weapons.... Of greatest interest to us is

cooperation in destroying the stockpiles of chemical weapons earmarked for that, and the navy's out-of-service nuclear submarines, of which many remain undestroyed even since Soviet times.... I want to note that the responsibility for eliminating these weapons lies with Russia itself. We have been engaged, are engaged and will continue to be engaged in the disposition of these weapons, and if our partners are willing to render assistance here, we will be grateful.[198]

In turn, the United States sets as its priority the disposition of strategic arms and the security of nuclear weapons and nuclear materials.

The difficulties are exacerbated by differences in legislation of the countries involved. In some cases, the obstacle was the lack of necessary legislation in Russia for regulating certain aspects of free foreign assistance. In addition, the legal structure for international cooperation by Russian nongovernmental organizations, including scientific groups involved in defense programs, is still in the process of maturing.

The Scale of the Problems and Allocated Resources

The continuous growth of expenditures for Cold War legacy assistance programs to Russia compared with the initial estimates raises concerns in the United States and some other donor states. For example, in 1999 the U.S. DOD stated that U.S. expenditures associated with the construction of a facility in Russia to store the highly enriched fissile materials obtained from dismantling Russian nuclear weapons would amount to more than $640 million—instead of the $275 million previously anticipated. In addition, the United States would have to spend another $650 million to prepare the materials for long-term storage. Therefore, the total potential U.S. expenditures for the design, construction, and transferring of materials to this storage facility may reach $1.3 billion. These expenses do not include the operational costs of the facility, which may exceed $10 million per year.[199]

Other examples of these kinds of high-cost projects that are favored by U.S. officials and lawmakers are the MPC&A program; the elimination of CW; and the implementation of the agreement concerning the disposition of 34 metric tons of Russian weapons plutonium. This poses the question of how the cost burden for the elimination of the Cold War legacy must be shared. Many donor states have grounds to believe that the growth in the cost of these projects is associated with the inability or reluctance of the Russian agencies to allocate the necessary funds, including funds agreed upon during the course of previous negotiations. This has raised the issue of what resources Russia can and must provide by itself in order to help eliminate the legacy of the Cold War.

---

198. Vladimir V. Putin (remarks at press conference following the G-8 summit, Kananaskis, Canada, June 27, 2002), www.mid.ru.

199. Harold J. Johnson, "Weapons of Mass Destruction: U.S. Efforts to Reduce Threats from the Former Soviet Union," testimony before the Subcommittee on Emerging Threats and Capabilities, U.S. Senate Committee on Armed Services, Report No. GAO/T-NSIAD/RCED-00-119 (Washington, D.C.: U.S. General Accounting Office, March 6, 2000), 4, www.gao.gov/new.items/n500119t.pdf.

Table 7.1. Outline of Proposed Spending over 8–10 Years, billions of U.S. dollars

Activities	Individual budget items	Subtotals	Total
Securing excess Russian plutonium		9.0	
Purchase and secure monitored storage of up to 100 metric tons	3.0		
Conversion of plutonium pits to oxide	1.0		
Immobilize or irradiate up to 100 metric tons	5.0		
Securing excess Russian HEU		11.0	
Purchase additional 200 metric tons HEU	4.0		
Downblend remaining excess HEU	7.0		
Improving security and accounting for nuclear material in Russia MPC&A improvements would include material consolidation; equipment upgrades; training of operators, managers, and regulators; computerized inventory systems; upgrading security during transport, etc.		5.0	
Downsizing and restructuring of Russia's excess nuclear complex		3.0	
Facility downsizing and preparation for civilian use	2.0		
Employ knowledgeable nuclear personnel	0.7		
Replace plutonium reactors	0.3		
Assure transparency in Russia and verify progress		2.0	
Estimated cost to achieve goals Benchmark: 1 percent current defense budget over this period			30.0

Source: Table prepared by Graham Allison, director of the Belfer Center at Harvard University and
is reproduced in Baker and Cutler, *A Report Card on the Department of Energy's Nonproliferation Programs with Russia,* Appendix A-1. The table "suggests an allocation of funding
for a program of this magnitude. It is not intended to be of budget quality, nor to imply that
the U.S. should be the sole provider of funds for such a program."

Total Costs of Eliminating the Cold War Legacy

Estimates of the financial expenditures necessary to implement the planned reformations in Russia's nuclear weapons complex may serve as a basis for the analysis of assistance programs to Russia for the next decade. Cost estimates in table 7.1, which has been prepared by an independent expert, substantially exceed official estimates for some of the programs. For example, the U.S. DOE has estimated total expenses through 2020 for the MPC&A programs as $2.2 billion,[200] but table 7.1, shows that these programs may cost up to $5 billion.

If estimates on table 7.1 are correct, the annual amount necessary to reform the Russian nuclear complex and ensure the safety and security of nuclear facilities, materials, and weapons should be about $3 billion. This is approximately three times more than has been appropriated annually by all the donor states in recent years and one-third more than was anticipated by the G-8 in June 2002 to assist the NIS.

There is no comprehensive analysis of the costs necessary to implement all other assistance programs to Russia. Estimates are only approximate and describe an order of expenditures for the next decade with an accuracy of up to $100 million, that is, within 10 to 15 percent of the total amount.

Cost estimates for the elimination of Russian CW must be significantly increased. In accordance with the Russian governmental program approved in the summer of 2001, the total costs to eliminate the Russian CW stockpiles are estimated to be about R93 billion (slightly more than $3 billion using the early 2002 exchange rate). Many experts believe that after taking into account the ruble's purchasing power the actual price may balloon up to $5–$6 billion. Therefore, in the coming decade the annual costs for these projects, on average, should be $300–$600 million.

Large expenditures will also be required to eliminate SSNs and SSGNs. From $400 million to $1 billion may be required for nonstrategic nuclear submarines that have yet to be decommissioned. In addition, the average annual maintenance costs may amount to $40–$100 million in addition to the U.S. funds already allocated to eliminate SSBNs.

It is possible to estimate roughly the costs for creating alternative jobs unrelated to military activities for scientists, engineers, and specialists formerly involved in the weapons sector. The cost to create one job in a nonmanufacturing business or in an industry related to information technologies—for example, software development—is about $10,000.[201] A similar amount may be required to retrain one individual. Therefore, the creation of new workplaces or the retraining for several dozen persons will require several hundred million U.S. dollars (at $10,000 per worker, $100 million will retrain 10,000 people). The costs will increase significantly, however, if it is necessary to employ some of these specialists in state-of-the-art industries where the creation of one workplace could cost several hundred thousand U.S. dollars or more.

The number of strategic carriers and the amount of missile fuel to be decommissioned in the coming decade are much more than what were eliminated in 1992–2000. This does not mean, however, that the costs of the elimination of strategic arms grows proportionally as the number of weapons and amount of fuel subject to elimination increases. Most of the funds provided in the form of assistance from 1992 to 2001 were used for the purchase of equipment and the construction of facilities, while the expenditures to be incurred during the coming

---

200. "Nuclear Nonproliferation: Security of Russia's Nuclear Material Improving; Further Enhancements Needed," Report No. GAO-01-312, 4.

201. Software development mainly requires providing the programmer with sufficiently powerful computers and a means of electronic communication—both of which are relatively inexpensive today.

decade will be primarily for operational costs. The issue of whether the donor states will finance operational costs is still open for debate, making it difficult to estimate with much precision the resources that will be necessary for the safe and secure elimination, storage, and transport of strategic offensive arms. Today we can only assume that in the next decade the costs will approximately equal those of the past five years: $100–$200 million per year.

Thus, a rough estimate shows that during the coming decade Russia and the donor states must jointly spend a total of at least $35 billion to eliminate threats associated with excess Russian WMD, related enterprises, and research institutions. This is significantly over and above the $20 billion committed by the G-8 member states for assistance to the NIS in the coming decade. It is overly optimistic to expect that the amount of external funding will show a significant increase. Such a situation makes the issue of how much Russia itself can allocate for these projects even more acute.

Russia's Share of the Costs

Insufficient financing of these programs by Russia is one of the most serious sources of resentment by the donor states. They are concerned that Russia often breaches its financial commitments, which leads to continual restructuring of the agreed programs and an increase in expenditures on the part of the partners. In particular, the United States has had to greatly increase its share of the burden for construction and operational support of the fissile material storage facility at PO Mayak after Russia stated that it was unable to pay its share of expenses. Russia's lament that its difficult economic situation prevents it from allocating resources to fulfill its international commitments—in this case, for the Mayak facility and for preparing the weapons-grade plutonium to be stored there—has become an annoyingly common refrain.

The displeasure displayed by the donor states seems to be well grounded. For example, the government of the Russian Federation decided that MINATOM would be the lead agency responsible for disposing of nuclear submarines. The program, jointly developed in 1999 by MINATOM and other federal executive bodies, predicted that through 2020, approximately R20 billion would be required for the disposal of retired SSNs and SSGNs and for the development of the needed onshore industrial infrastructure. In 2000, however, government funding provided only about 8 percent of the total amount needed for that year. About half the amount that MINATOM spent on these programs was earned through its external economic activities.

The situation concerning the elimination of CW is even more illustrative. According to official Russian government data, until 2001 when the updated federal program was approved, R1,263.4 million (in 2001 prices), or somewhat more than $40 million, had been spent. This was about 1.5 percent of the total program budget. At the same time, according to official data from the donor states, the total foreign funding for Russian programs for the elimination of CW reached $300 million.

The information available does not allow for a more exhaustive assessment of the situation regarding Russian financing for its part in these programs. Only a part

Table 7.2. Expenditures of the Russian Ministry of Defense, including Implementation of International Arms Control Agreements, 1994–2002, in billions of rubles

Categories of expenditures	1994	1995	1996	1997	1998	1999	2000	2001	2002
Expenditures of Russia's Ministry of Defense (A)	37.7	53.2	68.4	88.3	79.4	91.6	137.7	203.1	263.8[a]
Expenditures incurred in the fulfillment of arms control agreements (B)	0.8	0.0	3.3	3.1	1.9	1.7	2.1	6.0	9.7[b]
(B) as a percentage of (A)	2.2	0.0	4.8	3.5	2.4	1.9	1.5	3.0	3.7

Sources: *SIPRI Yearbook 2000: Armaments, Disarmament, and International Security* (in Russian) (Moscow: Nauka, 2001), 298; *SIPRI Yearbook 2001: Armaments, Disarmament and International Security* (Oxford: Oxford University Press, 2001), 314.

a. Expenditures for armed forces maintenance and development.

b. Expenditures for arms dismantlement to comply with international arms control agreements.

of the funds appropriated in the federal budget for these purposes is actually spent on these programs, and the agencies responsible for these programs may seek additional financial sources. On the whole, Russian funding efforts in this area have been minimal. For example, the portion of Russia's budget allocated for the implementation of international arms control agreements, primarily for the elimination of excess armaments, from 1996 to 2000 steadily decreased as part of Russia's total defense expenditures. This trend reversed only in 2001. In fact, in 1996–1997, to fulfill its part of the international arms control agreements, Russia spent about $500 million annually (per the exchange rate of that period). These expenditures decreased to $60–$70 million by 1999–2000, but they increased to $200 million in 2001, and to approximately $300 million in 2002.

In 1996 and 1997 Russia did fulfill its agreements to spend $500–$600 million a year; therefore one may conclude that such a level of funding is economically acceptable for Russia. This is about 0.5 percent of Russia's total export revenues and about 1.5 percent of all federal expenditures.

Between 1999 and 2002, in spite of its difficult economic situation, Russia's military budget grew by more than R170 billion, almost a threefold increase (table 7.2). At the same time, the amount set aside for fulfilling international commitments regarding arms control increased by only R8 billion.

In this situation it is important to achieve a clear-cut agreement between Russia and the donor states regarding the size and form of the Russian contribution to financing the Cold War legacy elimination programs. Russia must make binding commitments and guarantee the allocation of resources within the agreed amounts.

Russia could take a somewhat different approach, however. Russia could make a commitment to allocate a fixed share of its military expenditures, for example, 5–10 percent. The absolute amounts allocated by the donor states and Russia to eliminate the Cold War legacy is an important factor—but not the only factor—for the success or failure of the programs. The effective use of the appropriated funds—a subject under serious political discussions—is just as important.

Procedures for Allocation and Use of Resources

On the Russian side, concern is frequently expressed, and not without reason, that the funds intended to assist Russia in eliminating its Cold War legacy are allocated annually and their availability may be withdrawn by a decision of the donor state's legislature. The U.S. Congress's decision in 2000 to suspend funding for the elimination of CW in Russia is an example. The Russian concern is that this current procedure for providing these resources does not allow for the creation of long-term plans for implementing the programs and projects that are intended to take several years to complete.

In addition, Russian experts and officials often comment that a great portion of the funds allocated for assistance to Russia is actually spent in the United States. Thus, it is frequently said that Russia receives only 20–40 percent of the appropriated funds while most are spent in the United States for organizational and technical activities. In addition, the U.S. agencies are reluctant to share with their Russian counterparts information on the expenditures incurred by the assistance program. Also, the Russian side is allowed little participation in deciding how outstanding issues are resolved.

Most likely these statements are only partially true. For example, the U.S. General Accounting Office in its 1999 report on the IPP revealed that about two-thirds of funds had been spent in the United States for managerial activities, financing of the U.S. laboratories, and taxes. Because of this, the U.S. Congress now requires that not more than 35 percent of the funds appropriated for this program can be spent in the United States.[202]

It is important to differentiate between two categories of expenses. The first consists of expenditures in the United States for organizational activities and certain work being done by U.S. organizations, the results of which remain in the United States. The second refers to payments for equipment manufactured by U.S. companies and supplied to Russia, for expert reviews necessary for the resolution of issues that are in some way related to the goals of the program, and so forth. Only the organizational-type of funds spent under the first category may be considered as not getting to Russia. The Russian agencies and industrial enterprises are of course interested in the bulk of the funds being spent in Russia. There is a certain logic in the conviction that Russian enterprises and design bureaus are more familiar with the specific conditions of Russian Cold War legacy issues and that the cost of comparable services and work in a number of cases is markedly lower in Russia than in the United States.

---

202. Amy F. Woolf, "Nuclear Weapons in Russia: Safety, Security, and Control Issues," CRS-11.

The persistent wish of the Russian agencies regarding the direct transfer of the majority of the funds to the Russian enterprises and organizations does not take into account the U.S. approach to assistance to Russia, however. The United States provides Russia with free assistance on certain terms and conditions and for resolving a specific range of tasks. In particular, the rendering of material resources, technical assistance, and training is intended to be supplied only through U.S. government contractors. This simplifies the authorization process for the U.S. Congress. Also, while disbursing free assistance to Russia, the U.S. administration has the legal and moral right to spend these funds as it deems legitimate. One can hardly object to the United States financing, as a first order of priority, projects that meet its national security interests, including those aimed at the elimination of surplus nuclear weapons in Russia.

Therefore Russia should not expect the United States to tackle the issue of financing housing in the satellite cities growing up near CW elimination enterprises or for retired military officers from the SRF and other units. U.S. legislation unambiguously prohibits the use of U.S. taxpayers' money to resolve such problems. A possible solution may be the use of nongovernmental funds from the donor states. A similar approach may be used to raise funds for retraining the retired military officers to ease their entry into the civilian sector.

Taxation Issues

Disagreements between Russia and the donor states have recently arisen with regard to the taxing of foreign legal entities and persons involved in assisting Russia in eliminating its Cold War legacy. This is due, in part, to the positions of Russia's Ministry of Taxes and Levies as well as the Ministry of Finance. They believe a 1992 U.S.-Russia agreement is no longer in force because the 1999 extension protocol of the agreement was not submitted to Russia's Duma for ratification within six months of signing, as required by Russian law. The two ministries therefore consider the assistance being rendered by the United States as subject to taxation.

Russia's Ministry of Foreign Affairs therefore believes that it must be guided by the provisions Russian federal law no. 101 of July 15, 1995, "On International Agreements of the Russian Federation" (Article 23, Paragraph 2), which states that the provisional application by the Russian Federation of an agreement is terminated when the other party is notified that the Russian Federation does not intend to become a party to the agreement. However, the Russian side did not send such a notification to the U.S. side. Therefore, whether an international agreement was submitted to the State Duma for ratification or not does not affect its provisional application.

The extension protocol to the 1992 agreement was not submitted for ratification because beginning in mid-2000, in response to a Russian government directive, various Russian ministries and agencies were undergoing a redistribution of responsibilities. This affected Russian agencies that had been the executive agents under the 1992 agreement. For example, the Ministry of the Economy, which had been the executive agent regarding elimination of the strategic offensive arms under the agreement, was abolished and its responsibilities were now given to MINATOM and Rosaviakosmos. The Russian Munitions Agency was put in charge of eliminating CW. This redefining of the responsibilities of various federal executive bodies, which has continued throughout the negotiations with the United States, is now close to an end. The poor coordination among the Russian governmental agencies as well as the negative political implications could well lead to a reduction in appropriations for Russian disarmament programs.

The Access Issue

One of the most acute and still unresolved issues, which creates substantial difficulties in implementing the assistance programs to Russia, is the issue of access to facilities where equipment received from the United States is installed or U.S. assistance is otherwise used.

U.S. government agencies, primarily DOE, as well as many prominent members of Congress believe that because the U.S. monitors are not granted access to a number of the facilities belonging to MINATOM, it is not possible to confirm that the financial resources and equipment provided by the United States are actually used for their designated purposes.

In turn, Russian officials believe that the U.S. agencies seek to obtain maximum information about the nuclear weapons facilities, the designers, and, if possible, the warheads themselves. To the Russian officials, verifying targeted use of the assistance is just a pretext. Russia's concern has been fueled by the large number of U.S. monitoring groups visiting the country and their unfixed composition, and Russia is concerned about the disclosure of extremely sensitive information. Russia therefore insists on rigorous guarantees that the classified information obtained in the course of the monitoring visits will not go beyond the restricted number of individuals directly involved in the implementation of the programs and projects.

On the whole, the issue of access to Russian nuclear weapons facilities is one of the most painful and intractable problems facing U.S.-Russia cooperation. It is unlikely that it will be fully resolved in the immediate future. It is important, however, to narrow the range of contradictions to the maximum extent—to shorten the list of facilities that under any conditions and terms will be closed to visits by foreign monitoring groups. Before Russia shortens its list of closed facilities, it will be necessary first to provide Russia with solid guarantees about the nondisclosure of confidential information and, second, to study the potential for indirect verification measures using equipment supplied by the United States.

Politicization of International Cooperation

In Russian political and scientific circles concern has been expressed that program assistance provided by the donor states, primarily the United States, is overpoliticitized. These Russian politicians and scientists see a direct link between financing for programs and Russian policy in certain areas of international relations. Their concern is likely well grounded, but there are two distinct aspects to the issue.

A number of the U.S. members of congress who are critical of assistance to Russia have sought to tie U.S. assistance to Russia's operations in Chechnya, the termination of Russia's nuclear cooperation with Iran, and other Russian policies.

Their proposals would be formulated by the U.S. Congress as nonbinding resolutions instead of amendments to the legislation.

In addition, U.S. legislation mandates that funds allocated for Cold War legacy programs and projects cannot be used for objectives other than those directly related to the goals of the specific programs. For example, such funds cannot be used for any peacekeeping activities, financing of housing, financing of environmental rehabilitation, or retraining of retired military officers.

These are political strings. They are the result of a complicated situation in the U.S. establishment in which the need to assist in the elimination of Russian WMD is not evident to all parties. The majority of U.S. lawmakers and leaders in the executive branch believe that the United States can and must help Russia where and when it directly corresponds to U.S. security interests, but that U.S. assistance should not be used to solve problems that Russia is capable of resolving on its own.

To a certain extent, these political terms and conditions incorporate the legal requirement that a recipient state is committed to:

- Investing a portion of its own resources for dismantling and eliminating WMD;

- Refraining from modernizing its armed forces if these forces exceed reasonable defense needs or if the modernization envisages the replacement of the WMD that have been destroyed;

- Refraining from using fissile materials and other components from decommissioned nuclear weapons to create new nuclear munitions;

- Providing the donor country with the opportunity to monitor operations related to the elimination of armaments for which the donor funds were allocated;

- Following all corresponding arms control agreements; and

- Respecting internationally acknowledged human rights, including minority rights.

It is difficult to contest the legitimate nature of these requirements. For example, it would be counterproductive if the United States agreed to assist a country in eliminating obsolete or unnecessary armaments, but that recipient country continued to build new armaments, did not follow signed arms control agreements, and so on. The only issue that seems unconnected with these provisions is the point concerning the respect of human rights. That point is of a strictly political nature, but it corresponds with the global trend of expanding the influence of democratic states and in no way retards the progressive transformation of the Russian political system.

Russia's Fulfillment of the CWC and BWC

Recently the scope of Russia's commitment to the CWC and the BWC has become an issue. President George W. Bush's administration has not seen a way to confirm to the U.S. Congress that Russia is fulfilling its international obligations. As a result, in 2002 all assistance channeled through DOD has been blocked. Basically, these problems have been brought about by the regrettable breach of treaties and agreements on arms control by the former Soviet military command. In the past, the USSR recklessly violated the Anti-Ballistic Missile Treaty when it started to construct an early warning radar station near Krasnoyarsk. In addition, it violated the provisions of the BWC that it had signed in 1972 when it continued to develop offensive biological military programs. This resulted in a lasting distrust of statements by the Soviet military—a situation inherited by the Russian military command. To resolve this dead-end situation, serious political decisions are required.

Disagreements regarding Russia's fulfillment of its commitments under the CWC, in substance, are based on the concern that Russian agencies did not declare all storage sites for CW and possibly underestimated Russian CW stockpiles. These accusations are primarily built on inconsistencies between Western estimates of the production capacities of the former Soviet CW production enterprises and the quantities located in the declared storage facilities, the quantities eliminated after January 1, 1977, and quantities dumped into the sea after January 1, 1985.[203] In other words, there is no way to guarantee that some stocks of CW are not present somewhere outside the declared storage locations or were not destroyed in an undeclared location after January 1, 1977. In fact, in June 2002 the U.S. military discovered vessels containing chemical agents (or that formerly contained chemical agents) that were left by Soviet troops at an airfield in Khanabad, Uzbekistan.[204]

Doubts regarding Russian fulfillment of its commitments under the BWC are a much more complicated situation. President Boris Yeltsin acknowledged officially in 1992 that, in spite of the obligation not to produce biological weapons, the former Soviet Union had pursued military biological offensive programs. Today the official Russian position on the issue has been reduced to the following points:

- Activities associated with the so-called offensive part of the military biological program are prohibited and were eliminated in 1992;

- So-called large-scale equipment was destroyed by order of Mikhail Gorbachev at the beginning of perestroika; work on destroying this equipment continued up until 1998;

- Since 1992 there has been continued elimination of laboratory-scale and large-scale testing equipment;

---

203. According to the CWC, a participating state must indicate the exact location, total quantity, and detailed inventory of the CW in its possession, ownership, or placed in any location under its jurisdiction or control. A participating state must also declare whether it left CW on the territory of other states. These provisions are not applicable if a participating state determines that the CW were buried on its territory before January 1, 1977, or dumped into the sea before January 1, 1985.

204. Yuri Chernogaev, "American Soldiers Find Soviet Chemical Weapons," *Kommersant*, June 11, 2002, p. 2; Bruce Pannier, "Uzbekistan: Discovery of Gases at Coalition Base Raises Questions," Radio Free Europe/Radio Liberty, June 11, 2002, www.rferl.org/nca/features/2002/06/11062002160455.asp.

- The storage process for biological weapons is very complex, and strategic stockpiles have not been created; and

- Military scientists work with agents that civilian scientists do not work with (Ebola, Marburg, and Lassa fevers) to create vaccines.[205]

The West, however, is not fully confident about Russian official statements. In particular, the West assumes that Russia still possesses equipment capable of producing large amounts of pathogens usable as weapons.[206] The West's distrust is amplified by the Russian authorities' refusal since the early 1990s to allow foreign experts into selected Russian facilities, facilities that the West believes can be put back into service if military offensive biological programs are resumed.

Insufficient Coordination

Another serious drawback affecting cooperation between Russia and the donor states is insufficient project coordination that leads to various bureaucratic obstacles that impede the decisionmaking process. Many Western experts believe that the most serious manifestation of inefficiency on the part of Russian government agencies is the slow process of negotiating and ratifying agreements regulating access to nuclear and other military facilities. In particular, negotiations concerning the MPC&A program dragged out for a very long time and stalled implementation.

The most important omission in the Russian mechanism for decisionmaking related to international cooperation to eliminate the Cold War legacy is the absence of a superagency capable of overcoming institutional interests, realizing Russian national interests, and promptly eliminating problems as they arise. To be effective, such a superagency would need to be headed by one of the vice prime ministers of the Russian government.

Russian experts and officials also complain that there is poor coordination among the various U.S. programs. This leads to duplication, dispersion, and a lack of a systematic approach. To Russia's irritation, the lack of interagency coordination also sometimes results in the establishment of U.S. assistance programs for the resolution of minor issues. Some Russian representatives express displeasure with the current practice of giving grants directly to Russian laboratories and scientists because the government is then deprived of an opportunity to influence the selection of research topics or have access to the results.

In light of the political commitments made at the G-8 meeting in mid-2002 to allocate $20 billion for the elimination of the Cold War legacy, improving international coordination among programs acquires the utmost importance. The G-8 recognized this when it decided to:

---

205. Valentin Yevstigneev, "Ebola Strain Was Brought to Russia by Spies," *Yaderny Kontrol* (in Russian) No. 4 (July–August 1999): 15–23.

206. See, for example, Michelle Stem Cook and Amy F. Woolf, "Preventing Proliferation of Biological Weapons: U.S. Assistance to the Former Soviet States," CRS Report for Congress, No. RL31368 (Washington, D.C.: Congressional Research Service, Library of Congress, April 10, 2002), 3–4.

...establish an appropriate mechanism for the annual review of progress under this initiative which may include consultations regarding priorities, identification of project gaps and potential overlap, and assessment of consistency of the cooperation projects with international security obligations and objectives. Specific bilateral and multilateral project implementation will be coordinated subject to arrangements appropriate to that project, including existing mechanisms.[207]

To ensure the effective functioning of this mechanism in Russia, special interagency or superagency authorities must be created in the United States and also in other donor states to integrate and coordinate efforts and programs and to overcome an overly institutionalized approach to examining disputed issues. Such authorities could also represent each of the countries internationally when cooperation efforts are under discussion.

Education about Nonproliferation and the CTR Program

Although there has been progress in eliminating WMD and WMD delivery mechanisms and in strengthening the physical protection of nuclear facilities, efforts undertaken in the field of education regarding nonproliferation under the CTR program have not been sufficient.[208] During the 1990s, the countries involved did not pay sufficient attention to the importance of the human factor in reducing WMD proliferation.

Since the early 1990s, more than 200,000 scientists have left Russia.[209] Because the Russian government does not have the means to provide its domestic scientists with a competitive salary, the only way to retain highly qualified specialists is to create a favorable environment by developing joint projects with Western colleagues. Simply raising salaries for Russian nuclear experts will not be enough; such a strategy reduces the risks but does not protect against the theft of sensitive materials and technologies or negligence when working with such materials.

Even the most generous investment in new technical means for protecting sensitive materials and weapons from unauthorized access and proliferation can guarantee success only when there is full-scale education and retraining of the personnel who have direct access to the given types of weapons, their components, and the corresponding technologies. This is also true for the general public. Such education, carried out primarily by mass media and nongovernmental organizations, must explain the principles and legal basis of the nonproliferation regime and

---

207. "The G-8 Global Partnership Against the Spread of Weapons and Materials of Mass Destruction," Statement of G-8 Leaders, June 27, 2002, www.g8.gc.ca/kan_docs/globpart-e.asp.

208. For details on nonproliferation education, see Anton Khlopkov, "Education in Disarmament and Nonproliferation: Time to Act," *Yaderny Kontrol* (in Russian) No. 4 (September–October 2002): 60.

209. "The state will provide science with money," *Ytro.Ru* (Internet news service; in Russian), March 19, 2002, www.utro.ru/articles/2002031913592267474.shtml.

describe possible implications if the nonproliferation principles and norms are violated or ignored.

The Russian government must also make a strong effort to continue the ongoing education of junior experts who have recently graduated from educational institutions and are now the employees of nuclear research centers, the Ministry of Defense, or the Ministry of Foreign Affairs and whose responsibility it is to deal with nonproliferation issues. The implementation of Russia's international nonproliferation and WMD elimination commitments will depend on them.

Although educational and advanced training programs in the field of WMD nonproliferation are rare, the United States and Russia are leading in the number of such programs. These two states still possess the largest stockpiles of nuclear weapons and fissile materials usable for military purposes; they also possess CW although they are reducing their numbers.

In 2002, a textbook on nuclear nonproliferation was published in Russia. Earlier, in 2001, the Russian Ministry of Education approved a new specialization to be taught in educational institutions: nonproliferation and security of nuclear materials. Advanced training and educational programs for different audiences—journalists, lawmakers, federal officers, nuclear scientists, customs officers, and teachers—have already been developed and implemented. Over the past five years, the Moscow Physics and Engineering Institute has offered a master's degree to specialists in the areas of nonproliferation, physical protection, control, and accounting of nuclear materials. An important element of the program is a series of lectures entitled "Nuclear Nonproliferation: International Legal, Economic, and Political Aspects," which has been developed and presented by experts from the PIR Center.

These advanced training programs are intended for customs and law enforcement officers as well as for specialists who have the direct access to sensitive technologies and materials. This program has been implemented and must be expanded. Educational efforts must be focused on students, postgraduates, and junior experts. Unfortunately, little has been done in Russia so far. Investments in the younger generation must be recognized as farsighted and strategic. It is necessary to expand the basic and advanced training programs in nonproliferation primarily through regional educational institutions. Many have already expressed such an interest: Kazan State University, Saint-Petersburg State University, Seversk State University, Tomsk Polytechnical University, Trekhgorny Institute of Technology, Urals State University, and Yaroslavl State University.

Key steps for creating and promoting a Russian nonproliferation educational program could include:

- Development of training materials on nonproliferation (primarily focused on but not limited to nuclear nonproliferation), including a general course for students in all educational institutions specializing in the area of nonproliferation and disarmament;

- Broad distribution, in both hard copy and electronic forms, of international treaties and agreements relating to the subjects of disarmament and nonproliferation;

- Preparation and dissemination of CD-ROM versions of the above training materials and documents among workshop participants such as journalists and students in advanced training courses;

- Development of disarmament and nonproliferation training programs for lecturers and instructors of fundamental and advanced training programs;

- Creation of easy-to-understand videos to promote the values of nonproliferation and disarmament; popularize these videos through workshops for TV journalists, nongovernmental organizations, and universities;

- Creation of remote education programs—an online series of lectures and virtual textbooks as well as online testing of the trainees' knowledge; and

- Stimulation of junior- and senior-year university students, graduate students, junior experts, and journalists working on the issue of WMD to broaden their interest in nonproliferation and disarmament.

Should these measures be implemented in an integrated step-by-step manner over several years, they would significantly reduce the threat of WMD proliferation.

Now that the United States and Russia have signed an agreement concerning new levels of strategic arms, educational issues in the field of disarmament and nonproliferation acquire special significance. It may sound paradoxical, but the absence or weakening of a national educational system in this area significantly increases the proliferation risk even while the number of nuclear weapons is being reduced.

Strengthening of the nonproliferation regime is acknowledged by the Russian leadership as a top-priority task for the country's national security, as mentioned in Russian national security concept documents.[210] The lack of educational programs in the field of nonproliferation is the weakest spot in the formation of a new culture in Russia, and this situation needs to be turned around. It is important to expedite measures to bridge this gap by implementing measures outlined in the framework of the CTR program.

The 2002 G-8 Summit and the Future of Nonproliferation Assistance to Russia

Decisions made during the G-8 summit in mid-2002 are a sign of the emerging international recognition of the need to assist Russia in dismantling its Cold War legacy. But the importance of those decisions is not limited to only the political commitment to raise up to $20 billion over the next decade. Priority areas of cooperation resulting from the G-8 summit include eliminating CW, dismantling nuclear submarines, disposing of nuclear materials, and placing scientists and spe-

---

210. "Russian Federation National Security Blueprint," approved by presidential decree no. 1300, December 17, 1997; and "National Security Concept of the Russian Federation," approved by presidential decree no. 1300, December 17, 1999 (as edited in presidential decree no. 24 of January 10, 2000), *Diplomaticheski Vestnik* No. 2 (2000): 3–13; see www.fas.org/nuke/guide/russia/doctrine/.

cialists formerly involved in military programs in new jobs. The ongoing work of the international community in these areas is to be intensified.

Of special importance has been the decision to create a mechanism for consulting on priorities, focusing on areas of deficiency or unnecessary duplication of work as well as developing a diagnostic tool for assessing correspondence among the cooperative efforts and international security commitments and problems.

Especially important is the possibility of coordinating key elements of the underlying legal foundation for cooperative efforts between Russia and developed democratic states:

i.   Mutually agreed effective monitoring, auditing and transparency measures and procedures will be required in order to ensure that cooperative activities meet agreed objectives (including irreversibility as necessary), to confirm work performance, to account for the funds expended and to provide for adequate access for donor representatives to work sites;

ii.   The projects will be implemented in an environmentally sound manner and will maintain the highest appropriate level of safety;

iii.   Clearly defined milestones will be developed for each project, including the option of suspending or terminating a project if the milestones are not met;

iv.   The material, equipment, technology, services and expertise provided will be solely for peaceful purposes and, unless otherwise agreed, will be used only for the purposes of implementing the projects and will not be transferred. Adequate measures of physical protection will also be applied to prevent theft or sabotage;

v.   All governments will take necessary steps to ensure that the support provided will be considered free technical assistance and will be exempt from taxes, duties, levies and other charges;

vi.   Procurement of goods and services will be conducted in accordance with open international practices to the extent possible, consistent with national security requirements;

vii.   All governments will take necessary steps to ensure that adequate liability protections from claims related to the cooperation will be provided for donor countries and their personnel and contractors;

viii.   Appropriate privileges and immunities will be provided for government donor representatives working on cooperation projects; and

ix.   Measures will be put in place to ensure effective protection of sensitive information and intellectual property.[211]

---

211. From "Kananaskis: Statement by G8 Leaders," http://www.g8.gc.ca/kananaskis/globpart-en.asp (accessed December 11, 2002).

Realization of these rules—especially agreements on access to sites, due privileges and immunities for foreign officials, and the protection of sensitive information and intellectual property—may facilitate effective international cooperation and mitigate existing differences between Russia and the donor states.

It was naïve to imagine that Russia would immediately receive $20 billion after the G-8 summit. In any case, these funds are not for use in Russia alone. Every G-8 state has been given the opportunity to join the G-8 Global Partnership against the Spread of Weapons and Materials of Mass Destruction established by the G-8 summit, and other countries are expected to join.

The assistance Russia is going to receive will likely not be only in the form of appropriated monies; it could include a swap of Russia's debts for nonproliferation measures that Russia itself completes. Other options are also possible. Russia will need to define clearly and coordinate with donor states the work that it is able to do independently.

Finally, the intention of presidents and prime ministers to grant aid to Russia does not guarantee that the funds will reach Russia. In democratic states the decision to allocate funds is made by the legislative bodies. Generally speaking, it is impossible to guarantee that requests for the allocation of funds will pass with ease through the parliaments of the G-8 countries.

Conclusions

International assistance allows Russia to fulfill its commitments under START I, including the construction of costly facilities necessary to destroy armaments and matériel and the implementation of programs to mitigate related environmental problems. Because of U.S. assistance, it has become possible within a short time to transfer from the NIS to Russia all the nuclear weapons that had been manufactured in the Soviet Union and ensure their safe and secure storage at bases operated by the Russian Ministry of Defense. This has reduced the risk of nuclear terrorism.

Issues related to the disposition of radioactive waste and spent nuclear fuel from decommissioned nuclear submarines have recently acquired a heightened level of importance. Elimination of the radioactive waste and spent fuel could take years without foreign assistance. The elimination of chemical weapons could be delayed. Thus, without massive external assistance, it is unlikely that Russia will be able to fulfill its commitments under the Chemical Weapons Convention within the established timelines. These commitments are additional to other pressing tasks that Russia would likely be unable to resolve independently.

However, the elimination of this legacy of the Cold War is a problem associated not only with Russia. It is one of the large-scale and important tasks the community of democratic countries is facing. The leaders of the G-8 states and their governments specifically linked the solution of these legacy issues to the prevention of proliferation of weapons of mass destruction and the means of their delivery as well as to combating international terrorism. Establishment of a global partnership to achieve this goal requires that leaders of the most influential states have the political will to carry out these deeds and efforts. To this end, it is necessary for Russia and the donor states to overcome a number of difficulties and disagreements and create efficient institutional mechanisms and interaction procedures.

In particular, it would be useful to set up an international agency uniting Russia, the United States, the European Union, Japan, and other leading donor states in order to coordinate international assistance to Russia. The primary tasks of such an agency could be to estimate the scale and nature of the problems Russia is facing and identify ways of solving them through long-term plans and programs. This mechanism could help Russia and the donor states find solutions to the most difficult problems that now impede cooperation between them. For example, agreement could be reached on the size of Russia's contribution to the joint efforts and, what is possibly more important, on the criteria determining that contribution; on joint development of principles, guidelines, and parameters regarding Russia's disclosure of information on its resources and efforts allocated for eliminating its Cold War legacy; and on methods of monitoring how funds channeled to Russia by the donor states are used. In turn, donor states should not seek to obtain excessive information and must guarantee confidentiality of information as necessary. This multilateral international mechanism could help in developing a sound legal basis for interaction between Russia and the donor states as well as for interaction among the donor states themselves. Such interaction would facilitate implementation of the agreed long-term programs and projects.

Difficulties of implementing joint programs and projects intended to assist in eliminating the Cold War legacy are to a great extent related to the lack of a super-agency capable of effectively coordinating the activities of the ministries and agencies that are involved in these international programs and efforts. This paper underlines the importance and necessity of setting up such a structure, which we believe could be headed by one of the vice prime ministers of the Russian Federation.

Difficulties in eliminating the Cold War legacy arise in Russia not only from the lack of resources in Russia but also because of disagreements with the donor states. Difficulties also result from the fact that foreign assistance is sometimes viewed as an additional source of funds to help enterprises, institutes, and ministries not only resolve issues related to the management of weapons and materials but also survive any current bureaucratic crises by directing their own resources to other purposes. In this regard, one of the most important tasks is to develop in Russia a culture of nonproliferation that is grounded in the belief that the proliferation of weapons of mass destruction is the most serious threat facing Russia's national security.

The ratification of the Vienna Convention on Civil Liability for Nuclear Damage is of practical importance. Also important is finding solutions to the issues of foreign assistance taxation and the related problem of taxation of profits of foreign companies assisting Russia in program implementation.

The most tangible results may be achieved by involving the international financial community. The best options for donor countries and international financial and credit organizations (such as the IMF, World Bank, and EBRD) may be supplying Russia with long-term, interest-free credits; channeling money to targeted programs from governmental and private funds; involving private and corporate investors; and/or restructuring and writing off Russia's existing debt to the donor states and major debenture holders (the G-7 states, major IMF members, the World Bank, the Paris Club, and the London Club) under the condition that the released funds will be used for disarmament programs.

Appendix

Table A.1. Funds Notified by the U.S. Congress for Nonproliferation Cooperation with Russia and NIS, as of September 30, 2000, millions of U.S. dollars

Funding	Russia	NIS excluding Russia	Subtotals	Totals
Funds budgeted in compliance with the Freedom Support Act (FSA)				
Department of Energy				
IPP	30.67	4.33	35.00	
Department of State				
Science centers	69.00	62.41	131.41	
Export control/border security	3.20	16.80	20.00	
CRDF	9.00	14.23	23.23	
U.S. Nuclear Regulatory Commission	13.88	22.08	35.96	
Total in compliance with FSA	**125.75**	**119.85**		**245.60**
Funds budgeted in compliance with other laws				
Department of Defense/CTR Program				
Weapons dismantlement	1,037.36	631.57	1,668.93	
Chain of custody	890.92	111.06	1,001.98	
Demilitarization	113.33	267.18	380.51	
Other	30	89.04	119.04	
Department of Defense/other programs				
Border and customs security/ counterproliferation	0.50	13.73	14.23	
DOD/FBI counterproliferation	0	5.35	5.35	
Subtotal DOD	**2,071.61**	**1,118.43**	**3,190.04**	
Department of Energy				
MPC&A	607.44	34.47	641.91	
IPP	111.06	12.43	123.49	

Funding	Russia	NIS excluding Russia	Subtotals	Totals
Export control programs (nuclear)	3.57	6.64	10.21	
Uranium supply enrichment	1.00	0	1.00	
Arms control support	55.06	18.38	73.44	
R&D	13.80	0	13.80	
Fissile materials disposition	232.20		232.20	
Nuclear Cities Initiative	20.00	0	20.00	
Reduced Enrichment for Research and Test Reactors (RETR)	2.32	0	2.32	
Subtotal DOE	**1,047.45**	**71.92**	**1,119.37**	
Department of State				
Nonproliferation, Anti-Terrorism, Demining, and Related Programs (NADR)/ Counterproliferation	7.95	5.95	13.90	
Nonproliferation and Disarmament Fund (NDF)	7.01	13.38	20.39	
Subtotal DOS	**14.96**	**19.33**	**34.29**	
CRDF	18.84	13.53	32.37	
Total budgeted, excluding FSA	**3,152.86**	**1,223.21**		**4,376.07**
Total FSA and non-FSA funds	**3,278.61**	**1,343.06**		**4,621.67**

Source: Based on "Cumulative Funds Budgeted (FY 1992 to date) for Major NIS Assistance Programs by Country as of 9/30/00 (millions of dollars, rounded to nearest $10,000)," www.state.gov/documents/organization/2378.pdf.

Table A.2. Funds Obligated by the U.S. Congress for Nonproliferation Cooperation with Russia and NIS, as of September 30, 2000, millions of U.S. dollars

Funding	Russia	NIS excluding Russia	Subtotals	Totals
Funds budgeted in compliance with the Freedom Support Act (FSA)				
Department of Energy				
IPP	30.67	4.33	35.00	
Department of State				
Science centers	69.00	62.41	131.41	
Export control/border security	3.20	16.80	20.00	
NSF/CRDF	6.65	5.37	12.02	
U.S. Nuclear Regulatory Commission	13.64	20.38	34.02	
Total in compliance with FSA	**123.16**	**109.29**		**232.45**
Funds budgeted in compliance with other laws				
Department of Defense/CTR Program				
Weapons dismantlement	769.89	565.53	1,335.42	
Chain of custody	680.21	109.12	789.33	
Demilitarization	103.79	252.51	356.30	
Other	30.04	85.93	115.97	
Department of Defense/other programs				
Border and customs security/ counterproliferation	0	12.74	12.74	
DOD/FBI counterproliferation	0	4.28	4.28	
Subtotal DOD	**1,583.93**	**1,030.11**	**2,614.04**	
Department of Energy				
MPC&A	579.18	18.07	597.25	
IPP	111.06	12.43	123.49	
Export control programs (nuclear)	3.57	6.64	10.21	
Uranium supply enrichment	1.00	0	1.00	
Arms control support	53.06	18.38	71.44	
R&D	13.80	0	13.80	

Funding	Russia	NIS excluding Russia	Subtotals	Totals
Fissile materials disposition	63.30	0	63.30	
Nuclear Cities Initiative	19.94	0	19.94	
Reduced Enrichment for Research and Test Reactors (RETR)	1.39	0	1.39	
Subtotal DOE	**846.30**	**55.52**	**901.82**	
Department of State				
Nonproliferation, Anti-Terrorism, Demining, and Related Programs (NADR)/ Counterproliferation	7.95	5.95	13.90	
Nonproliferation and Disarmament Fund (NDF)	7.01	13.38	20.39	
Subtotal DOS	**14.96**	**19.33**	**34.29**	
CRDF	15.97	11.03	27.00	
Total budgeted, excluding FSA	**2,461.16**	**1,115.99**		**3,577.15**
Total FSA and non-FSA funds	**2,584.32**	**1,225.28**		**3,809.60**

Source: Based on "Cumulative Funds Budgeted (FY 1992 to date) for Major NIS Assistance Programs by Country as of 9/30/00 (millions of dollars, rounded to nearest $10,000)," www.state.gov/documents/organization/2378.pdf.

Table A.3. Funds Disbursed by the U.S. Congress for Nonproliferation Cooperation with Russia and NIS, as of September 30, 2000, millions of U.S. dollars

Funding	Russia	NIS excluding Russia	Subtotals	Totals
Funds budgeted in compliance with the Freedom Support Act (FSA)				
Department of Energy				
IPP	30.51	4.19	34.70	
Department of State				
Science centers	67.87	48.17	116.04	
Export control/border security	—	—	—	
CRDF	4.53	3.69	8.22	
U.S. Nuclear Regulatory Commission	13.13	16.87	30.00	
Total in compliance with FSA	**116.04**	**72.92**		**188.96**
Funds budgeted in compliance with other laws				
Department of Defense/CTR Program				
Weapons dismantlement	520.46	462.02	982.48	
Chain of custody	401.92	106.33	507.55	
Demilitarization	99.00	237.06	336.06	
Other	28.30	65.86	94.16	
Department of Defense/other programs				
Border and customs security/ counterproliferation	0	12.74	12.74	
DOD/FBI counterproliferation	0	4.28	4.28	
Subtotal DOD	**1,049.68**	**887.59**	**1,937.27**	
Department of Energy				
MPC&A	513.04	17.72	530.76	
IPP	69.35	9.05	78.40	
Export control programs (nuclear)	3.57	6.41	9.98	
Uranium supply enrichment	1.00	0	1.00	
Arms control support	52.26	10.8	63.06	
R&D	13.80	0	13.80	

Funding	Russia	NIS excluding Russia	Subtotals	Totals
Fissile materials disposition	44.30	0	44.30	
Nuclear Cities Initiative	16.94	0	16.94	
Reduced Enrichment for Research and Test Reactors (RETR)	1.39	0	1.39	
Subtotal DOE	715.65	43.98	759.63	
Department of State				
Nonproliferation, Anti-Terrorism, Demining, and Related Programs (NADR)/ Counterproliferation	3.80	4.53	8.33	
Nonproliferation and Disarmament fund (NDF)	7.01	13.38	20.39	
Subtotal DOS	10.81	17.91	28.72	
CRDF	15.39	10.53	25.92	
Total budgeted, excluding FSA	1,791.53	960.01		2,751.54
Total FSA and non-FSA funds	1,907.57	1,032.93		2,940.50

Source: Based on "Cumulative Funds Budgeted (FY 1992 to date) for Major NIS Assistance Programs by Country as of 9/30/00 (millions of dollars, rounded to nearest $10,000)," www.state.gov/documents/organization/2378.pdf.

Table A.4. Nuclear Submarines Built in USSR/Russia, 1958–2001

Project	NATO class	Type	No. built	No. of reactors	Total reactors in class	Vessels still in operation	
						Northern Fleet	Pacific Fleet
First generation							
627 A	November	SSN	13	2	26	0	0
658	Hotel	SSBN	8	2	16	0	0
659/675	Echo I/II	SSGN	34	2	68	0	0
Second generation							
667 A	Yankee	SSBN	34	2	68	1	0
667 B-BDRM	Delta I-IV	SSBN	43	2	86	10	6
670	Charlie I-II	SSGN	17	2	34	0	0
671 RT/RTM	Viktor I-III	SSN	48	2	96	8	2
Third generation							
941	Typhoon	SSBN	6	2	12	3	0
949/A/	Oscar I-II	SSGN	13	2	26	5	5
945	Sierra	SSN	4	1	4	3	0
971	Akula	SSN	13	1	13	6	7
Fourth generation							
935	Borei	SSBN	Under construction	1	1	0	0
705	Alfa	SSN	7	1	7	0	0
Prototypes							
645 ZhMT	November design	SSN	1	2	2	0	0
661	Papa	SSGN	1	1	1	0	0
685	Mike	SSN/SMS	1	1	1	0	0
885	Severod-vinsk	?	Under construction	1	1	0	0
Minisubmarines							
10831		SMS	1	1	1	?	?
1851	X-ray	SMS	1	1	1	?	?
1910	Uniform	SMS	3	1	3	?	?
Total			**248**		**465**	**36**	**20**

Source: Based on "The Arctic Nuclear Challenge," Report No. 3 (Oslo: Bellona Foundation, June 2001), www.bellona.no/en/international/russia/waste-mngment/21133.html.

Acronyms

AECL	Canadian Atomic Energy of Canada, Ltd.
AIDA-MOX	France-Russia research program to study use of uranium and plutonium
AMEC	Declaration on Arctic Military Environmental Cooperation
BIS	Bureau of Industry and Security, U.S. Department of Commerce
BWC	Biological Weapons Convention
C&A	control and accounting
CANDU	Canadian deuterium-uranium reactors
CATF	closed administrative-territorial formations
CFE	Conventional Armed Forces in Europe
CIS	Commonwealth of Independent States
CITS	Center for International Trade and Security, University of Georgia
CPSU	Communist Party of the Soviet Union
CRDF	Civilian Research and Development Foundation
CTR	cooperative threat reduction
CW	chemical weapons
CWC	Chemical Weapons Convention
DEK	Department of Export Control
DOD	U.S. Department of Defense
DOE	U.S. Department of Energy
DOS	U.S. Department of State
EBRD	European Bank for Reconstruction and Development
ENCI	European Nuclear Cities Initiative
EU	European Union
FAPRID	Federal Agency for the Protection of State Intellectual Property
FISCANM	Federal Information System for Control and Accounting of Nuclear Materials
FMSF	fissile material storage facility
FSA	Freedom Support Act
FSB	Federal Security Service

FY	fiscal year
G-8	Group of Eight
Gosatomnadzor	Federal Nuclear and Radiation Safety Authority
GRS	Society for Reactor Safety (Germany)
GSPI	Federal Special Design Institute of MINATOM
GTK	State Customs Committee
HEU	highly enriched uranium
IAEA	International Atomic Energy Agency
ICBM	intercontinental ballistic missile
ICP	internal compliance program
IMF	International Monetary Fund
INF	irradiated nuclear fuel
IPP	Initiatives for Proliferation Prevention
IPPE	Institute for Physics and Power Engineering
ISTC	International Science and Technology Center
LRW	liquid radioactive waste
MCC	Mining and Chemical Combine
MEDT	Ministry of Economic Development and Trade
MEPhI	Moscow Engineering Physics Institute
MINATOM	Ministry of Atomic Energy
MOX	mixed oxide
MPC&A	Materials Protection, Control, and Accounting
MTCR	Missile Technology Control Regime
NADR	Nonproliferation, Anti-Terrorism, Demining, and Related Programs
NCI	Nuclear Cities Initiative
NDF	Nonproliferation and Disarmament Fund
NIS	newly independent states
NNSA	National Nuclear Security Administration, DOE
NPO	scientific industrial association
NPP	nuclear power plant
NPT	Nuclear Non-Proliferation Treaty
NTI	Nuclear Threat Initiative
NWC	nuclear weapons complex
OKBM	Special Design Bureau for Mechanical Engineering
OPCW	Organization for Prohibition of Chemical Weapons

RANSAC	Russian-American Nuclear Security Advisory Council
RETR	Reduced Enrichment for Research and Test Reactors
RFNC	Russian Federal Nuclear Center
RIAR	Research Institute for Atomic Reactors
RMTC	Russian Methodological and Training Center on Nuclear Materials Control and Accounting
Rosaviakosmos	Russian Space Agency
RRC	Russian Research Center
RW	radioactive waste
SCC	Siberian Chemical Combine
SCTR	Strengthening Cooperative Threat Reduction
SLD	Second Line of Defense
SRF	Strategic Rocket Forces
SRW	solid radioactive waste
SSBN	nuclear-powered capable of launching ballistic missiles
SSGN	nuclear-powered submarine capable of launching guided missiles
SSN	nuclear attack submarine
TACIS	Technical Assistance in the Commonwealth of Independent States
TN VED	customs code number
USEC	United States Enrichment Corporation
USSR	Union of Soviet Socialist Republics
VNII	All-Russian Research Institute
VNIIAES	All-Russian Research Institute of Nuclear Power Plants
VNIIEF	All-Russian Research Institute of Experimental Physics
VNIITF	All-Russian Research Institute of Technical Physics
WMD	weapons of mass destruction

About the Authors

VITALY FEDCHENKO is a PIR Center project coordinator and junior research associate. He defended his master's thesis at the faculty of physics and economics of high technologies at the Moscow Engineering Physics Institute (MEPhI) in 2002. Currently he coordinates CTR research and outreach projects of the PIR Center, and his research interests include general issues of CTR, nuclear submarine dismantlement, and nuclear proliferation in South Asia.

YURI FEDOROV is a professor and a PIR deputy director. His specialty is international security, arms control, and political decisionmaking. He has written widely on strategic offensive weapons, tactical nuclear arms, missile defense, and early warning systems. Prof. Fedorov has edited and contributed to the annual UNDP human development reports; publications on Russia-NATO relations, the impact of recent elections on U.S. foreign policy, and Russia-Europe relations for a project by the Swedish National Defense College; and publications on energy security issues. Prof. Fedorov also participated in the program on post-Communist security studies at King's College, London. After graduation from the Physical Faculty of the Moscow State University, Prof. Fedorov served at the Institute of Sociological Studies of the Soviet Academy of Sciences and as head of a section in the Department of Disarmament Studies of the Institute of World Economy and International Relations. He also served in the International Department of the Central Committee of the CPSU and in 1991 became deputy chair of the Department of Political Science in the Moscow State Institute of International Relations (MGIMO). In December 2000 Prof. Fedorov became director of the Strategic Studies Department of the Institute for U.S. and Canada Studies. Since 1997 he has been member of the PIR Center executive board.

ANTON KHLOPKOV is a PIR Center educational project director. His academic specialization was Russian-Iranian nuclear energy cooperation and nonproliferation, and his research interests include regional aspects of WMD nonproliferation. He is the author of articles in Russian and in English in *Russian Security, Yaderny Kontrol Digest*, and *Nezavisimoye Voennoye Obozreniye*. He is a coauthor of *Nuclear Nonproliferation in U.S.-Russian Relations: Challenges and Opportunities*.

ELINA KIRICHENKO received a doctorate from the Moscow State University in 1963 and since 1968 has served with the Institute of World Economy and International Relations (IMEMO) of the Russian Academy of Sciences. Since 1995 she has headed the Center for North American Studies at IMEMO. She is a member of research councils at IMEMO and the PIR Center and is a member of the Institute of Nuclear Materials Management.

DMITRY KOVCHEGIN is a PIR Center research associate and a graduate of the MEPhI. His current research interests include the nonproliferation aspects of nuclear material management and nuclear technologies.

VASILY LATA, a reserve lieutenant general, is a senior adviser of the PIR Center as well as a professor, with a doctorate in military science, at the Military Science Academy. After a long and varied military career—General Lata was the first deputy to the chief of the military policy directorate and the head of the operational directorate and first deputy to the head of the Strategic Missile Forces supreme staff—that included international training at Harvard University, Gen. Lata is now senior research associate at the Peter the Great Strategic Missile Forces Military Academy and a professor at the General Staff Academy. He has experience in the conceptualization, application, and reformation of Russia's strategic missile forces and armed forces.

VLADIMIR A. ORLOV is the founding director of the PIR Center. Dr. Orlov currently directs the Center's Nuclear Nonproliferation and Russia Program and is the editor in chief of the Center's journal on international security, arms control, and nonproliferation, *Yaderny Kontrol* (Nuclear control). Dr. Orlov consults with the United Nations on nonproliferation education and is a professor at the MEPhI. His international experience includes membership on the Russian Pugwash Committee; research at the Center for Nonproliferation Studies, Monterey Institute of International Studies; and membership in the core group on nuclear nonproliferation at the Monterey Institute. Dr. Orlov was also the vice president, a member of the board of directors, columnist, political analyst, and head of department for *Moskovskiye Novosti* (Moscow News) from 1990 to 1996. Dr. Orlov defended his dissertation in political science and graduated from the MGIMO. He has published both in the West and in Russia; his publications include *Export Controls: Policies and Practices, Nuclear Nonproliferation* (a textbook), and *Nuclear Nonproliferation in U.S.-Russian Relations: Challenges and Opportunities* (2002), of which he was both editor and coauthor.

VALERY SEMIN is the principal adviser for the Department for Security and Disarmament Affairs of the Russian Ministry of Foreign Affairs. As a doctor of technical science, professor, and corresponding member of the Russian Academy of Natural Sciences, Dr. Semin has served as the vice head of department for the Russian Agency for Intellectual Property (1990–1992) and as scientific adviser to the Russian Consulate General in San Francisco (1993–1997). He is a graduate of Tula State University, Birmingham University, and the supreme diplomatic courses of the diplomatic academy of Russia's Ministry of Foreign Affairs. Dr. Semin is the author of 40 research papers, and he holds 15 patents. He is a member of the PIR Center research council.

PIR Center for Policy Studies

The PIR Center is a nonprofit, independent, Moscow-based research and public education organization that was founded in April 1994. The PIR Center's activities include research, publishing, information and consulting services, and education in accordance with Russian legislation.

The Center is currently focused on international security, arms control (primarily nuclear weapons), and nonproliferation issues that are directly related to Russia's internal situation, its national interests, security, and role in the international community.

The PIR Center has a staff of 25 as well as more than 60 contributors engaged in 20 short-term and long-term projects. The first project of the Center was the publication of the journal, *Yaderny Kontrol,* launched in 1994. Also since 1994 the PIR Center has published its *Security Issues Newsletter.* In June 2001, the PIR Center began publication of *Missiles and Outer Space Newsletter.*

As Russia's leading nongovernmental research institution in the area of nonproliferation, the PIR Center includes Russian and foreign experts in its activities and maintains close and continuing contacts with Russia's executive and legislative branches. The audience for the Center's academic and technical journals and reports includes Russian policymakers, legislators in the federal assembly, and other experts as well as the decisionmaking communities of other countries in the CIS. Most of its study papers and reports are in Russian.

PIR Center research associates participated in the 1995 and 2000 NPT Review Conferences as nongovernmental organization representatives. In 1999–2000, the PIR Center conducted a poll, "Russians on Nuclear Weapons and Nuclear Threats," and in 2000 the Center published the first comprehensive Russian textbook on nuclear nonproliferation. In 2000, the PIR Center and the Carnegie Moscow Center cohosted the Moscow International Nonproliferation Conference, which brought together 205 delegates from 24 countries, including Israel, India, Iran, and Cuba.

The PIR Center has a dynamic and developing Web site (www.pircenter.org) containing most of its publications. The PIR Arms Control Library holds a vast collection of books, journals, newspapers, and documents, including files on specific research topics. The Center has developed the YADRO (Nuclear Russia) database, which comprises materials on nuclear arms, nuclear policy, nuclear safety and security, nuclear materials and their physical protection, accounting and control, spent nuclear fuel, nuclear export, export controls, unauthorized access to nuclear materials, nuclear terrorism, nuclear technologies, and dual-use technologies.

The PIR Center's educational and training programs are recognized internationally; the Center's director, Vladimir Orlov, has been appointed UN consultant on disarmament and nonproliferation education and training.